The
ULTIMATE
Pumpkin
COOKBOOK

By

FRAN HORAN

8028 *Wichita Street* #78
Fort Worth, Texas 76140
817-615-4878
E-mail: forchava@yahoo.com

Editor	Fran Horan
	Jeff Kleemeyer
Photography	Fran Horan
	Betty Cho
	Amanda Rollins
	Jessica Binion
Graphic Design	Betty Cho
Original Artwork	Fran Horan
Art Direction	Betty Cho
	Fran Horan

© *2006 By Su-Chava Publications*
8028 Wichita Street #78
Fort Worth, Texas 76140
817-615-4878
E-mail: forchava@yahoo.com

Table of Contents

IV

Preface

Almost every Cook has tried their hand at making a pumpkin pie. It's simple; just follow the directions on the back of the label on the can of pumpkin. As far as fresh pumpkins go, well you know those end up on the curb, where they worked their way from the front porch, and have melted wax candle inside. If the pumpkin is lucky and has responsible owners, they proudly become Zoo food! I want to challenge you to step out of the ordinary and do something different. Be brave; make pumpkin soup!

Of course there are pumpkin pie recipes in my cookbook, lots of them in fact, but you will also find recipes for soup, muffins, bread, candy, cookies, and even pumpkin as a side dish. If you are really want to show some culinary skill, try serving pumpkin as a main dish. You can't create a more attractive dinner presentation than an oven baked pumpkin full of meat and rice, or soup served in a Pumpkin Tureen.

The recipes in this book come from all over the world. The foreign measurements have been carefully adjusted to American equivalents of the typical volume form of measurements such as cups, teaspoons and tablespoons. I could not have done this without out the help of my friends who learned to cook using measurements of weights. Thanks Sam and Raymond!

Some of the directions have been rewritten and recipes in every category have been tested with the goal to make them easier to understand and accommodate cooks at any level of experience. I have also made an effort to keep the entire recipe on one page, however, there are a few that extend over to next page. It is always a good practice to read through a recipe thoroughly before beginning and mentally work your way through all of the procedures, while making sure you have all of the ingredients. Pumpkin is very versatile and there is a lot of room for substitutions as well as creativity.

I believe this to be a much needed and equally wanted cookbook with hopes that it helps reduce the waste of all of this beautiful fruit wasted every fall. Take advantage of this wonderful and delicious fall produce and turn that jack-o'-lantern frown into a smile while you bring out the gourmet cook in you.

Dedication

I wish to dedicate <u>The Ultimate Pumpkin Cookbook</u> to the memory of my daughter, Tracy Nadine Rollins (Cook), whose love of the pumpkin inspired this work. Shortly Tracy and her husband, James Cook, bought their first home, one of the first honey do's she doled out to him was to prepare a pumpkin patch beside the house. On the south side of the house there was a narrow space that was virtually useless but the soil was rich and had good light.

She thought he knew everything there was to know about gardening because he was a foreman for a landscaping company. I guess he did, because that patch produced pumpkins year after year. In fact, that pumpkin patch produced a lot of pumpkins over the years, until she suddenly passed away at the early age of 27.

The fall of 1998 was the last harvest in Tracy's pumpkin patch. Her husband and their sons couldn't bring themselves to pick Tracy's pumpkins that year. They were hers to pick, so they watched the flowers bloom and the pumpkins grow until the Colorado snow came and covered them. The freezer was still full of pumpkin from last years crop, and the year before, and maybe even the year before that.

Tracy's love of pumpkin went beyond planting, growing and cooking. She also collected pumpkin figurines and made ceramic pumpkins. One of her children's most prized keepsakes is a cute ceramic jack-o'-lantern that sits unfinished on the shelf all year around.

To my surprise, as I prepared the work for this book, I discovered that there are many who share her love for this funny looking fruit. They are quite pretty, but most of all, they taste real good. One thing about Tracy, she was very curious, wondering if you could do more than just make pies and jack-o'-lanterns out of pumpkins.

Sorry it took me so long, but, yes Tracy, there are more to the pumpkin than pies, jack-o'-lanterns, and zoo food.

In loving Memory
Mom

VI

History of the Jack-o'-lantern

Making jack-o'-lanterns at Halloween came from a centuries old Irish myth about a man called Stingy Jack. According to the legend, Stingy Jack invited the Devil for a drink, which he didn't want to pay for when finished. He talked the Devil into turning himself into a coin to pay for their drinks. He then put the coin into his pocket along side a coin with a cross on it, to keep the Devil from changing back.

Eventually, Jack freed the Devil after making him promise not to bother him for a whole year and if Jack died, he wouldn't claim his soul. When the next year came around, Jack tricked the Devil again. This time he tricked him into climbing a tree to pick a piece of fruit. While the Devil was in the tree, Jack carved a cross into the tree's bark so the Devil couldn't come down until he promised not to bother Jack for ten more years.

Ten years didn't pass before Jack died. As the legend goes, God would not let Jack into heaven, being the unsavory character that Jack was. The Devil, still upset with Jack because of the tricks he had played on him, and keeping his word not to claim Jack's soul, wouldn't allow him into hell. Having the last laugh, the Devil sent Jack into the dark night with one burning coal to use for light, which he put into a carved out turnip and has been roaming the Earth with it ever since. The Irish began to refer to this ghostly figure as "Jack of the Lantern," and then, simply "jack-o'-lantern."

In Ireland and Scotland, people made lanterns by carving scary faces into turnips or potatoes and placing them in windows or near doors to run off Stingy Jack and other evil spirits. England uses large beets. Immigrants from these countries brought the jack o' lantern tradition with them when they came to America, but soon found that pumpkin, a fruit native to America, made perfect jack-o-lanterns.

Tips & Facts

In the Beginning

Pumpkin comes from the Greek word for "large melon" which is "pepon." Nasalized by the French, "Pepon" became "pompon." The English changed "pompon" to "Pumpion." Shakespeare referred to the "pumpion" in his *Merry Wives of Windsor*. American colonists changed "pumpion" into "pumpkin." The "pumpkin" is referred to in classic literary works such as: <u>The Legend of Sleepy Hollow</u>, <u>Peter, Peter, Pumpkin Eater</u> and of course, <u>Cinderella.</u>

Buying the Perfect Pumpkin

In America, the most popular use of pumpkins is for decoration during Halloween as jack-o'-lanterns, but the pumpkins use goes far beyond snaggletooth grins glowing on the front porch. When selecting a pumpkin for cooking, the best selection is a "pie pumpkin" or "sweet pumpkin." These are smaller than the large jack-o'-lantern pumpkins and the flesh is sweeter and less watery. However, you can substitute the jack-o'-lantern variety with fairly good results.

Look for a pumpkin with 1 to 2 inches of stem left. If the stem is cut down too low, the pumpkin will decay quickly or may be already decaying at the time of purchase. Avoid pumpkins with blemishes and soft spots. It should be heavy; shape is not very important unless you plan on using your pumpkin to serve your dish in. A lopsided pumpkin is not necessarily a bad pumpkin. Figure one pound of raw, untrimmed pumpkin for each cup finished pumpkin puree.

Preparing Pumpkin

Spread newspapers over your work surface. Start by removing the stem with a sharp knife. If you are planning to roast the pumpkin seeds, smash the pumpkin against a hard surface to break it open. If not, cut in half with a sharp knife. In any case, remove the stem and scoop out the seeds and scrape away all of the stringy mass. A messy job, but it will pay off.

Cooking Pumpkin
Boiling or Steaming Method

Cut the pumpkin into rather large chunks. Rinse in cold water. Place pieces in a large pot with about a cup of water. Water does not need to cover the pumpkin pieces. Cover the pot and boil for 20 to 30 minutes or until tender, or steam for 10 to 12 minutes. Check for doneness by poking with a fork. Drain the cooked pumpkin in a colander. Reserve the liquid to use as a base for soup. Follow the steps outlined below in 'Preparing the Puree'. During the cooking phase, the pulp will turn a dark brown. The pulp puree should be used within 36 hours.

Oven Method

Cut pumpkin in half, scraping away stringy mass and seeds. Rinse under cold water. Place the pumpkin with the cut side down on a large cookie sheet. Bake at; 350°F for one hour or until fork tender. Then follow the procedure outlined below in 'Preparing the Puree'.

Microwave Method

Cut pumpkin in half, place cut side down on a microwave safe plate or tray. Microwave on high for 15 minutes; check for doneness. If necessary continue cooking at 1-2 minute intervals until fork tender. Continue as outlined below in 'Preparing the Puree'.

Preparing the Puree

When the pumpkin is cool enough to handle, remove the peel using a small sharp knife and your fingers. Put the peeled pumpkin in a food processor and puree or use a food mill, ricer, strainer, or potato masher to form a puree.

Pumpkin Nutrition Facts

(1 cup cooked, boiled, drained, without salt)

Calories	49.0	Zinc	1.0	mg
Protein	2.0 grams	Selenium	.50	mg
Carbohydrate	12.0 grams	Vitamin C	12.0	mg
Dietary Fiber	3.0 grams	Niacin	1.0	mg
Calcium	37.0 mg	Folate	21.0	mg
Iron	1.4 mg	Vitamin A	2650.0	IU
Magnesium	22.0 mg	Vitamin E	3.0	mg
Potassium	564.0 mg			

Pumpkin Nutrients

	Raw (DB) 1/2 (cup)	Cooked (DB) 1/2 (cup)	Canned (DB) 1/2 (cup)	Libby's Canned 1/2 (cup)
Wt/svg (g)	58.0	122.5	122.5	122.0
Kcal (svg)	15.1	24.5	41.7	40.0
Fat(g)	0.06	0.09	0.34	0.5
Cholesterol (mg)	0.0	0.0	0.0	0.0
Carbohydrate (g)	3.8	6.0	9.9	9.0
Fiber (g)	0.29	1.3	3.6	5.0
Sodium (mg)	0.58	1.2	6.1	5.0
Potassium (mg)	197.2	281.8	252.4	n/a
Protein (g)	0.58	0.88	1.3	2.0
Vitamin A (IU/svg)	928.0	1325.5	27018.6	17500.0
Vitamin A (%RDI)	18.6	26.5	540.4	350.0
Vitamin C (mg/svg)	5.2	5.8	5.1	4.8
Vitamin C (% RDI)	8.7	9.7	8.5	8.0
Calcium (mg/svg)	12.2	18.4	31.9	40.0
Calcium (% RDI)	12.0	1.8	3.2	4.0
Iron (mg/svg)	0.46	0.7	1.7	1.8
Iron (% RDI)	2.6	3.9	9.4	10.0
Folate (mcg/svg)	9.4	10.4	15.1	n/a
Folate (% RDI)	2.4	2.6	3.0	n/a

Freezing

Pumpkin freezes well. To freeze, measure cooled puree or cubes into cup portions, place in ridged freezer containers, leaving 1/2-inch headspace, or pack into zip closure bags. Label, date and freeze at 0° F for up to one year. Use puree in recipes or substitute in the same amount in any recipe calling for solid pack canned pumpkin. However, pumpkin is highly perishable and must be cooked the same day it is cut open. Otherwise, orange flesh will develop a feathery black mold.

Canning Pumpkins-Cubed

QUANTITY

An average of 16 pounds are needed per canner load of 7 quarts; 10 pounds are needed per canner load of 9 pints 2-1/4 pounds per quart.

QUALITY

Pumpkins should have a hard rind and string-less, mature pulp of ideal quality for cooking fresh. Small size pumpkins (sugar or pie varieties) make better products.

PROCEDURE

Wash; remove seeds, cut into 1 inch-wide slices and peel. Cut flesh into 1-inch cubes. Boil 2 minutes in water. CAUTION: DO NOT MASH OR PUREE. Fill hot jars with cubes and cooking liquid, leaving 1-inch headspace. Adjust lids and process. For making pies, drain jars and strain or sieve cubes.

Recommended Process Times for Pumpkin in a Dial-Gauge Pressure Canner

Style of Pack	Jar Size	Process Time	Canner Pressure (PSI) at Altitudes of			
			0 to 2000 ft.	2001 to 4000 ft.	4001 to 6000 ft.	6001 to 8000 ft.
Hot	Pints	55 min	11 lb.	12 lb.	13 lb.	14 lb.
Hot	Quarts	90 min	11 lb.	12 lb.	13 lb.	14 lb.

Recommended Process Times for Pumpkin in a Weighted-Gauge Pressure Canner

Style of Pack	Jar Size	Process Time	Canner Pressure (PSI) at Altitudes of		
			0 to 1000 ft.	Above 1000 ft.	
Hot	Pints	55 min	10 lb.	15 lb.	
Hot	Quarts	90 min	10 lb.	15 lb.	

Meat
&
Main Dish

1

Baked Pumpkin with Peach Filling

10 to 12 lbs. pumpkin
1/2 cup butter, softened
2 Tablespoons olive oil
2 lbs. course ground meat
1 cup onions, chopped

1/2 cup green peppers, chopped
1/2 teaspoon garlic, chopped
4 cups stock
1/2 cup Sherry
3 medium tomatoes, chopped

FILLING

1/2 teaspoon dried oregano
1 bay leaf
1 teaspoon salt
Cayenne pepper to taste
Freshly ground pepper

1 LB sweet potatoes, cubed
1 LB white potatoes, cubed
1 LB zucchini, sliced
3 ears corn, sliced 1inch rounds
4 fresh peaches, diced

Preheat the oven to 375° F. Scrub the outside of the pumpkin under cold running water with a stiff brush. With a large, sharp knife, cut down into the top of the pumpkin to create a lid 6 or 7 inches in diameter. Leave the stem intact as a handle. Lift out the lid and, with a large metal spoon, scrape the seeds and stringy fibers from the lid and from the pumpkin shell. Brush the inside with the soft butter.

Place the pumpkin in a large shallow roasting pan and bake in oven for 45 minutes, or until somewhat tender. The pumpkin shell should remain firm enough to hold the filling without collapsing. Meanwhile, heat the oil over moderate heat in a heavy skillet, adding meat; brown well, turning frequently. Then with a slotted spoon, transfer the meat to a platter.

Add a 1 teaspoon oil to oil remaining in the pan, add onions, green pepper and garlic, and cook over moderate heat, stirring constantly, for about 5 minutes, or until the vegetables are soft but not brown. Pour in stock and Sherry and bring to a boil over high heat. Scrape in any brown bits clinging to the bottom and sides of the pan. Return the meat and any of its juices to the pan and stir in the tomatoes, oregano, bay leaf, salt and a few grindings of black pepper. Cover and reduce heat to low, simmering for 15 minutes. Then add the sweet potatoes and white potatoes, cover and cook for 15 minutes; add the zucchini slices, cover again and cook for 10 minutes. Finally add the corn rounds and peaches and cook, still covered, for 5 minutes longer.

Pour contents of the pan carefully into the baked pumpkin, cover the pumpkin with its lid again, and bake for another 15 minutes in a 375° F oven. To serve, place the pumpkin on a large serving platter and, at the table, ladle from the pumpkin onto heated, individual serving plates.

Dinner in a Pumpkin

Med. sized pumpkin (4 LB)
1- 1/2 LB lean ground beef
1/3 cup chopped green pepper
1 (4-oz.) can mushrooms
3/4 cup chopped onion
1 teaspoon salt

1/4 teaspoon pepper
1/4 cup soy sauce
3/4 cup chopped celery
1 can cream of chicken soup
2 cups cooked rice

Using a sharp knife, cut lid from pumpkin and scoop out pumpkin seeds and excess membrane. In a large skillet, combine ground beef, chopped green pepper, chopped celery, and chopped onion. Cook over medium heat until ground beef is browned. Add next seven ingredients to skillet. Mix well and place mixture into pumpkin cavity. Place lid on pumpkin then put pumpkin on a foil-lined cookie sheet and bake at 350° F. for 1-1/2 hours. To serve, scoop out part of the baked pumpkin, along with the meat mixture, onto each plate.

Eighty percent of the pumpkin supply in the United States is available in October.

Sea Bass with Peppers & Pumpkin Seed Salsa

1 cup fresh or frozen corn kernels
6 tomatillos, diced
1/2 teaspoon cumin
Salsa
6 Chilean sea bass fillets (6-8 oz. each)
1 red bell pepper, roasted, peeled, seeded, cut in strips
1 poblano chili, roasted, peeled, seeded and chopped

Juice of 1 lime
1 cup toasted pumpkin seeds
Salt and pepper to taste

Prepare 2 hours before needed. Combine the corn, tomatillos, pumpkin seeds, and poblano chili. Season with the lime juice, cumin, salt and pepper. Set aside in the refrigerator for 2 hours. Season fish lightly with salt and pepper and grill, (can be broiled or baked) until done. Serve with the salsa and garnish with roasted pepper strips.

Roast & Pumpkin Australia Style

Lamb or beef roast
Medium size pumpkin, cubed
4 potatoes, quartered

2 cups baby carrots
1 stalk celery, sliced
Salt and pepper to taste

Seer all edges of roast until brown in pan suitable for pot roast. Cover with water, adding salt and pepper. Cook uncovered on medium high. After 30 minutes, add potatoes, carrots and celery. Add 2 to 3 cups pumpkin chunks to pan and cook with meat about one hour, then remove pumpkin with slotted spoon. Spread pumpkin pieces on a baking sheet and bake at 300° F. for about an hour. As roast cooks, do not replace water, letting it cook down. Serve with the roast and other vegetables.

Argentinean Stew in a Pumpkin Shell

2 lbs. beef stew meat
1 large onion; chopped
2 garlic cloves; minced
3 Tablespoons oil
2 large tomatoes; chopped
1 large bell pepper; chopped
Salt, pepper
1 teaspoon sugar

1 cup dried apricots
3 white potatoes, peel and diced
3 sweet potatoes, peel and diced
2 cups beef broth
1 medium pumpkin
Butter or margarine; melted
1/4 cup dry sherry
1 can whole kernel corn, drained

Trim any excess fat from beef and cook with onion and garlic in oil until meat is browned. Add tomatoes, green pepper, 1 tablespoon salt, 1/2 teaspoon pepper, sugar, apricots, white potatoes, sweet potatoes and broth. Cover and simmer 1 hour. Meanwhile, cut top off pumpkin and discard. Scoop out seeds and stringy membrane. Brush inside of pumpkin with butter and sprinkle lightly with salt and pepper. Stir sherry and corn into stew and spoon into pumpkin shell. Place shell in shallow pan and bake at 325° F 1 hour, or until pumpkin meat is tender. Place pumpkin in large bowl and ladle out stew, scooping out some of pumpkin with each stew serving.

In colonial New Haven, Connecticut, cut pumpkins were used as guides for haircuts to ensure a round uniform style. Because of this fashion, New Englanders were nicknamed "pumpkin-heads."

Persian Pumpkin Stew

1 LB stew meat (lamb or beef)
1 medium size pumpkin
1/2 cup dried prunes
3 Tablespoons tomato paste
Pinch saffron dissolved in

1 teaspoon turmeric
1/8 teaspoon cinnamon
1/2 chopped medium onion
Salt and pepper to taste
1/4 cup warm water

Sauté onion. Brown stew meat and add about 1-1/2 cups water. Add tomato paste, turmeric, cinnamon, saffron, salt and pepper and sautéed onion. Cover and simmer for about 1-1/2 to 2 hours. Meat should be tender and nearly falling apart. Add water during cooking if needed.

Seed and clean pumpkin and slice into 2 x 2 inch pieces and peel. Brown on both sides in corn oil. The pumpkin should become brown in some places and somewhat flexible but not totally cooked. Add to meat and cook, covered an additional 20 to 30 minutes until tender but not falling apart. A fork should go into the pumpkin easily but not break it up. Add the prunes the last 5 minutes of cooking.

Hidatsa Stuffed Sugar Pumpkin

1 sugar pumpkin, 4-5 pounds
2 teaspoons salt
1/2 teaspoon dry mustard
2 Tablespoons butter
1 lbs ground buffalo, or other meat

1 medium onion, chopped
1 cup cooked wild rice
3 eggs, beaten
1 teaspoon crushed, sage
1/4 teaspoon pepper

Preheat oven to 350° F. Cut the top off, of the pumpkin and remove strings and seeds. Reserve seeds for another use. Prick the cavity with a fork and rub with 1 teaspoon salt and mustard. Heat butter in a large skillet, add meat and onion and sauté over medium-high heat until browned. Turn off the heat, stir in wild rice, eggs, remaining salt, sage and pepper. Stuff pumpkin with meat and rice mixture. Place 1/2 inch water in the bottom of a shallow baking pan. Put pumpkin in the pan and bake for 1-1/2 hours, or until tender. Add more water to the pan as necessary to avoid sticking. To serve, cut pumpkin into wedges, giving each person pumpkin and stuffing,

Smoked Turkey Pumpkin Stew

1 LB fresh pumpkin, seeded
1 teaspoon cumin seed
2 LB smoked turkey, cubed
2 Tablespoons flour
1 large onion, minced
3 cloves garlic, minced
1 teaspoon oregano
10 cups or so water

2 bay leaves
1 small bell pepper, minced
1 jalapeno, minced
1/4 cup chopped fresh cilantro
1 can white hominy, drained
Salt and freshly ground pepper
Fresh cilantro leaves

Preheat oven to 350° F. Arrange pumpkin skin side up in large baking pan. Add water just to cover bottom of pan. Cover and bake until pumpkin is tender and fork pierces center easily. Cool. Peel and cut into 3/4 inch cubes.

Toast cumin seed in small skillet over medium heat until fragrant, shaking pan constantly, about 3 minutes. Using spice grinder or mortar and pestle, finely grind cumin.

Heat 3 tablespoons butter in a large saucepan, over medium heat. Toss turkey cubes with flour. Add to pan in batches cooking until brown, returning all turkey to pan when finished. Add onion, garlic, oregano and cumin and cook until onion is soft, stirring frequently. Add 10 cups water and bay leaves and bring to boil. Reduce heat and simmer 30 minutes.

Add bell pepper, jalapeno and 1/4 cup chopped cilantro. Cover partially and simmer another 10 minutes. Stir in pumpkin, and hominy and cook 5 minutes. Season with salt and pepper.

Pumpkin Lamb Stew Over Rice

1 teaspoon cumin seeds	1 clove
2 Tablespoons vegetable oil	2 lbs. lamb stew meat
1 large onion, minced	4 cloves garlic, minced
2 carrots, cut into 1inch chunks	1 celery root, chunks
4 large, ripe tomatoes	1 acorn squash, cubed
2 quarts beef broth	1 large pumpkin, 5 lbs.
1 cup uncooked Basmati rice	1/2 teaspoon salt
1 teaspoon ground pepper	1 /4 cup coriander leaves
3/4 cup parsley, minced	

1/2 teaspoon each, coriander seeds, cardamom seeds, ground cinnamon

Combine coriander, cardamom, cinnamon, cumin and clove in a spice mill or coffee grinder grinding until smooth. Set aside. Heat 1 tablespoon of oil in large saucepan; add lamb and spice mixture, searing over medium heat until lightly browned. Remove lamb from pan and set aside.

Add the onion and garlic to the pan and sauté until translucent. Add the carrots, celery root, tomatoes, and acorn squash. Add the broth and return lamb to the pan. Partly cover and gently simmer until the lamb is tender, about 1-1/2 to 2 hours. Season; with salt and pepper.
Meanwhile, preheat oven to 350° F. Cut top of pumpkin and remove seeds. Place the pumpkin on a baking sheet Brush the outside with the remaining oil. Bake until tender, about 45 to 60 minutes. Cook the rice according to package directions, set aside.

To assemble, place the pumpkin in a serving dish. Fill with the lamb stew. Divide the rice among 4 warmed bowls. Ladle the stew from the pumpkin over the rice. Garnish with coriander and parsley.

Pumpkins range in size from less than a pound to over 1,000 pounds.

Pumpkin & Steak Stew

1- 1/2 lbs. beef round, cubed
1 Tablespoon butter
1 medium onion, chopped
2 stalks celery, chopped
5 cups water
1/2 teaspoon salt

1/2 teaspoon thyme leaves
1/4 teaspoon back pepper
1- 1/2 lbs. pumpkin
1/4 cup sifted all purpose flour
1 cup frozen green peas

In a 4-quart soup pot, brown beef in butter. Add onion and celery, sauté until browned. Stir in 4 cups water, salt, thyme, and pepper, heat to boiling. Cook covered 1 hour. Cut 2 inches off the top of the pumpkin. Trim edge of pumpkin to make zigzag shape, scoop out seeds. Peel top and trimmings and cut into 1 inch cubes, add to beef after 1 hour. Cook 30 minutes longer or until tender. Heat oven to 350° F. Bake pumpkin shell 20 minutes. Stir flour into 1 cup water, add stew with peas. Cook, stirring until thickened, spoon into shell and serve.

Chili Pumpkin Style

2 cups fresh canned pumpkin
3 lbs. lean ground beef
2 cans red kidney beans
2 medium onions, chopped
3 15 oz. cans cut tomatoes
2 Tablespoons chili powder

1/4 teaspoon red pepper
2 Tablespoons sugar
1 teaspoon salt
2 bay leaves
1 cup mushrooms

Brown ground beef and drain off excess fat. Put ground beef into a large pot. Add rest of the ingredients into the pot and cook on low for one to two hours. Serve with crackers.

Chicken Pumpkin Chili

2 Tablespoons olive oil
2 cups onion, chopped
2 cups bell pepper, chopped
3 Tablespoons jalapeno, minced
1 lbs. boneless, skinless chicken
   breasts, cubed
1 clove garlic, minced
1 cup beer
1 Tablespoon cocoa powder
1/4 cup ripe olives, sliced

1 teaspoon ground coriander
1/2 teaspoon salt
29 oz. canned tomatoes
   with juice, chopped
2 cups cooked pumpkin,
   peeled, cubed
2 Tablespoons cilantro, chopped
1 cup chicken broth
16 oz canned pinto beans, drained
3 Tablespoons chili powder

GARNISH
1-1/2 oz cheddar cheese, shredded
6 Tablespoons scallions, sliced Sour cream

Heat oil in a Dutch oven or heavy soup pot, over medium heat. Sauté onions until lightly browned, then add bell pepper, jalapeno and garlic. Sauté for 5 minutes longer., add beer, broth, olives, chili powder, coriander, salt, tomatoes and chicken. When the mixture comes to a boil, reduce heat, covering partially; simmer for 15 minutes. Stir in the pumpkin, cilantro, cocoa and beans. Cook for 5 minutes.

Pumpkin Burgers

1-1/2 lbs. ground beef
1 medium onion, chopped
12 oz jar of chili sauce
1/2 cup pumpkin puree

1 teaspoon salt
1 teaspoon pepper
1 teaspoon pumpkin pie spice
1 can tomato soup

Combine ground beef and onion and brown lightly, breaking up meat with a fork. Add remaining ingredients. Cover and let simmer approximately 20 minutes; uncover and simmer 15 minutes longer until mixture is thick. Serve on buns.

Pumpkin Succotash with Dried Beans

1 cup chicken broth	2 tablespoon minced marjoram
1 teaspoon freshly ground pepper	1/2 teaspoon salt
1/4 teaspoon red chili flakes	1 teaspoon canola oil

1/4 cup dried black beans, soaked overnight and drained
1/4 cup kidney beans, soaked overnight and drained
1/4 cup dried pinto beans, soaked overnight and drained
1/2 cup dried lima beans, soaked overnight and drained
1/2 cup pureed tomatoes, strained
1 small pumpkin, peeled, seeded, and diced
2 cups chicken meat, pre cooked
1 cup fresh coriander leaves (cilantro)

Combine the beans, pureed tomatoes, pumpkin, chicken broth and marjoram in a large saucepan. Cook over medium heat, stirring frequently until the beans are tender, about 45 minutes. Season with salt and pepper. Meanwhile, combine the chili flakes and oil in a large cast iron skillet. Heat until smoking, add the chicken. Sauté over high heat until cooked through. Stir the chicken in the simmering stew.

Pumpkin on the Side

Vegetable Side Dishes

Candied Pumpkin

10 cups pumpkin, cubed   2 cups sugar

Place pumpkin in a large casserole dish. Cover with sugar and bake at 350° F. oven until pumpkin starts to get soft. Bake until liquid is the consistency of syrup.

Pumpkin with Sage

1-1/5 lbs. Pumpkin   8 fresh sage leaves
7 Tablespoons butter   Salt
1 white onion, sliced thin   White Pepper
3/4 cup freshly grated parmesan cheese

Peel pumpkin and remove all seeds and strings. Cut into finger width slices. Set aside. In a large skillet, over medium heat: melt half the butter and sauté onions, until translucent. Add pumpkin; raise heat and cook, stirring often until tender. Melt the rest of the butter and fry the sage leaves until crisp. At the same time, cook tagliatelle (fettuccine) or spinach fettuccine until al dente, and drain. Pour pumpkin sauce over pasta. Add cheese and pepper. Pour sage and butter sauce and toss. Serve hot.

Steamed Pumpkin

1-1/2 lbs. pumpkin   1 Tablespoon maple syrup
1/4 teaspoon mace   1/2 teaspoon salt
1/4 teaspoon allspice   2 teaspoons melted butter
1 teaspoon ground cardamom   Black pepper to taste

Cut pumpkin in half, scrape out seeds and fiber. Cut into 2 x 2 inch pieces. Steam 30 minutes or until tender. Cool slightly, and slip skin off pieces. Spoon pumpkin flesh into a food processor with remaining ingredients and process until smooth.

Pumpkin Gnocchi

1 small pumpkin, cut in pieces
1/2 cup semolina flour
1/2 to 1 cup potato flour, sifted
Parmesan cheese, freshly grated

Salt and white pepper
Nutmeg
1/4 pound unsalted butter

Preheat oven to 350° F. Place pumpkin in a shallow baking dish, skin side up, pour 3 tablespoons water into dish and bake until tender. Remove from the oven and cool. Peel off the skin and any burnt surfaces, then mash the flesh or put it through a food mill to yield 2 cups of pulp. Put pumpkin in a large bowl, season and begin to work in the flours. Use all the semolina and as much potato flour as is needed to make a soft easy to knead dough. Add salt, pepper, and nutmeg and knead lightly until elastic. Cover and rest for 10 minutes.

Break off little pieces about 3/4 inch long. Roll the pieces to obtain a smoother surface, then press them with your thumb, just below the top of the fork. Pull down toward the fork's handle and allow the dough to roll over on itself. To shape the gnocchi, hold a fork with the top side facing you. The pieces should have ridges on one side formed by the tines of the fork and a depression on the other, by your finger. While working with gnocchi, dust your hands and work surface regularly with flour. Dust lightly with potato flour and rest for 10 to 12 minutes, placing on a lightly floured surface.

Melt butter in a saucepan and cook over a medium heat until golden brown. Keep warm. Cook the gnocchi, a few at a time, in boiling salted water. When they rise to the surface remove with a slotted spoon and transfer to warm bowls. Pour the butter over the top, sprinkle on some Parmesan and serve immediately.

Garlic Butter Topping

1/3 cup butter, melted
6 to 7 finely chopped sage leaves

1 large clove garlic, minced
Parmesan Cheese, freshly grated

Melt butter in a small sauce pan. Add garlic and let cook for a minute. Turn offbeat and add sage.

Futari (Coconut-Peanut Pumpkin)

2 cups pumpkin, peeled & cubed
2 cups sweet potatoes, cubed
3 Tablespoons onion, finely chopped
1 Tablespoon oil
Juice of 1/2 lemon

1/2 teaspoon cloves
1 teaspoon salt
1-1/2 cup coconut milk
1 teaspoon cinnamon

Fry onion in oil until golden. Combine with pumpkin and the sweet potatoes in a heavy pot Add lemon juice, cloves, salt and 1 cup coconut milk. Cover and simmer for 10 minutes. Uncover, stir gently, adding cinnamon. Cook 15 to 20 minutes longer, stirring often to prevent sticking. Add more milk if necessary.

Baked Buttered Pumpkin

1 Pumpkin, cut into sections.
1/4 stick Butter

Black Pepper to taste

Preheat oven to 425° F. Cut pumpkin into sections and lay pumpkin on a piece of foil.

Add a couple pats of butter and lots of pepper. Wrap sections in foil and cook until tender. Scoop out and serve or mash.

Penne For Two with Pumpkin Sauce

1 onion, chopped fine
1 red bell pepper, chopped fine
2 garlic cloves, minced
2 Tablespoons butter
1/2 cup solid-pack pumpkin
1 cup chicken broth

1/2 cup water
2 Tablespoons heavy cream
Freshly grated nutmeg to taste
1/2 lb. penne, or tubular pasta
3 Tablespoons parsley, minced
Freshly grated Parmesan

In a large skillet, cook onion, bell pepper, and the garlic in butter over moderate heat until the vegetables are softened. Stir in the pumpkin, broth, water, cream, nutmeg, salt and pepper to taste. Simmer the sauce, stirring occasionally, for 10 minutes.

While the sauce is simmering, in a kettle of salted boiling water boil the penne until it is al dente. Reserve about 1 cup of the cooking water, and drain the penne well. Add the penne to sauce, cooking the mixture over moderate heat for 1 to 2 minutes, or until the pasta is coated well,. Stir and thin the sauce as desired with some of the reserved cooking water. Stir in parsley. Divide the pasta between 2 plates and serve it with the Parmesan.

Pumpkin, Rice & Apricots

3 Tablespoons oil
1 medium onion, chopped
6 cups pumpkin, cubed
3/4 cup dried apricots, chopped

1 teaspoon salt
3/4 cup water
1 cup cooked rice

Heat the oil in a large skillet over medium heat. Add onion and sauté, until it begins to brown. Add pumpkin pieces to skillet, stirring to coat. Add apricots, salt and 3/4 cup water. Cover and simmer for 15 minutes. Add cooked rice and cook 10 minutes, or until pumpkin is tender. Stir often as it cooks.

Saged Pumpkin Sauce Over Pasta

1 cup heavy cream
1/2 cup pumpkin puree
1/4 cup fresh-grated Parmesan
16 leaves fresh sage

1/2 teaspoon salt
1/4 teaspoon ground pepper
1 Tablespoon butter
1 package cooked pasta

Combine the cream, pumpkin puree, parmesan, sage, salt and pepper in a medium saucepan over medium heat. Simmer the mixture until slightly thickened, about 10 to 12 minutes. Remove from heat and stir in butter. Toss with cooked pasta and serve immediately.

Wild Rice Stuffed Pumpkins

STUFFING
1/2 cup wild rice
1 teaspoon olive oil
1 clove garlic, minces
1 chicken bullion cube
Water

1/8 cup angel hair pasta,
pinch basil, thyme, oregano
1 branch parsley, chopped
1 can cream of mushroom soup
1 pumpkin

Bake pumpkin halves in a 375° oven, upside down in a pan with a little water for 20 minutes. Turn them right side up and finish for 10 minutes more, until tender but not dried out, .in a hot skillet, lightly scorch rice and angel hair pasta, broken into small pieces, in olive oil. Add garlic and herbs, then cover with water, throwing in bullion cube. Cook on medium heat until rice is tender and water is absorbed. Stir in mushroom soup straight from can, do not dilute. Stuff the pumpkin cavity full, packing it down. Press buttered bread crumbs on top. Heat thoroughly, in an oven over hot water (about 10 minutes).

Holiday Stuffed Pumpkin

1 10 inch pumpkin with stem	1/2 teaspoon ground cinnamon
2 cups brown rice	1/4 teaspoon ground nutmeg
1 cup other whole grains	1/4 teaspoon ground cloves
(barley or millet)	1 cup cooked garbanzos
2 teaspoons olive oil	1 cup roasted chestnuts
1/2 cup chopped onion	1/2 cup raisins or cranberries
3/4 cup chopped celery	1/2 cup chopped pine nuts
2 cups sliced apples	1/4 cup chopped parsley
1 sweet red pepper, chopped	black pepper to taste
1 teaspoon dried sage	3 Tablespoons orange juice,
1/2 teaspoon dried thyme	frozen
8 oz extra sharp cheddar, grated	

Preheat oven to 400° F. Carefully cut the top off the pumpkin with a knife angled toward the center of the pumpkin so the lid won't fall in when baked. Clean seeds and strings out of the center and put a couple of tablespoons of water into it, oiling the cut edges of both pumpkin and lid. Bake both parts on a baking sheet for about 40 minutes, or until the pumpkin is quite soft when poked with a fork. While the pumpkin is baking, cook the grains as usual.

Sauté the onion until translucent, then add the apples, celery, chestnuts, herbs and spices, and cook until the apples are just starting to get soft. Mix in beans, raisins, nuts, parsley, orange, and sweet red pepper, Heat gently. Add grains and mix well.

After the pumpkin is baked, stuff with fillings. If using cheese, layer stuffing and cheese, ending with cheese. Replace lid tightly. Lower the oven temperature to 350° F. and bake on a baking sheet for about 30 minutes, or longer, until stuffing is hot. Serve the stuffing with a slice of pumpkin topped with a bit of maple syrup, cranberry sauce or a fruit chutney.

Thanksgiving Pumpkin Stuffed with Rice & Chestnuts

1 medium pumpkin
2 Tablespoons honey
2 Tablespoons soy sauce
1 cup water
1/2 pound fresh chestnuts
1/4 cup un-sulfured raisins
1 red apple, chopped
1/4 cup diced celery
1 medium onion, chopped

2 ears corn kernels cut off cob
1 medium green pepper, chopped
2 cups cooked brown rice
1 lb. firm tofu, diced and drained
   paprika
1/4 teaspoon mace
3 Tablespoons mild soy sauce
1/4 teaspoon cinnamon
   parsley springs to garnish

Preheat oven to 350° F. Wash pumpkin and cut off the top. Use large spoon to scoop out strings and seeds. Mix honey and soy sauce and spread evenly over insides of pumpkin. Place 1 cup water in the bottom of large baking pan, place top back on pumpkin and place pumpkin in baking pan, cover with foil. Bake for 20 minutes or until pumpkin is just starting to become tender.

Meanwhile, prepare the chestnuts by cutting off the shells using a sharp knife. Chestnuts have a soft brown skin under the shell. Steam for about 15 minutes, or until tender. Rinse nuts in cool water and slip off skins then chop coarsely. Combine chestnuts with raisins, apple, celery, onions, corn, green pepper and brown rice, mix well.

Heat some water in medium skillet. Add tofu and enough paprika to give it a pleasing color and cook over high heat for 3 minutes, stirring constantly. Combine tofu with rice mixture, mace, and cinnamon and mix until well blended.

Fill the pumpkin with this mixture, replace top, place in baking dish with 1/4 inch water in bottom. Bake for 45 minutes; serve on large platter garnished with parsley, raw cranberries, and orange slices.

Elegant Stuffed Pumpkin

1 5 lb. pumpkin
3 cups brown rice, cooked
1 cup chopped celery
2 apples, tart, unpeeled, chopped

1 onion, chopped
2 cups wheat Bread crumbs
1 cup roasted chestnuts

HERBS
1 to 2 cups vegetable stock   1/4 to 1/2 cup butter,
1 teaspoon each sage, savory, marjoram, oregano, paprika, salt to taste.

Cut off top of pumpkin to make a lid. Remove the seeds and scrape out any stringy pulp. Combine dry ingredients in a large mixing bowl and mix well. Add stock and butter, and mix well, adding salt if desired. Stuffing should be moist but not wet. Pack loosely into pumpkin, replace lid, and bake on oiled cookie sheet for 1-1/2 hours or more at 325 ° F. It is done when a fork pushes easily through the pumpkin. Transfer pumpkin to a casserole dish and serve at the table, scooping out some of the tender pumpkin flesh with each serving of stuffing.

Stuffed Pumpkin

1 small pumpkin
2 Tablespoons butter
1 cup chopped onion
1 cup chopped celery
1/2 cup chopped green pepper
2 garlic cloves, minced
1-1/2 lbs. ground beef
1 can stewed tomatoes

6 carrots, sliced
5 potatoes, cubed
1 teaspoon Oregano
1 teaspoon parsley
1 Tablespoon Worcestershire sauce
1 cup grated cheddar cheese
   salt and pepper

Preheat the oven to 350° F. Wash pumpkin, cut off the top and scrape out seeds with membrane. Score pumpkin flesh on the inside, but do not pierce through the shell. Bake for 30 minutes. Meanwhile, sauté the onions, celery and green pepper in butter until tender. Add meat, tomatoes, carrots and potatoes. Season with oregano, parsley, pepper and Worcestershire sauce, simmer 15 minutes. Stuff the pumpkin with the meat mixture. Bake at 350° F. for 15 minutes. Sprinkle on the grated cheese and bake another 5 minutes.

Pumpkin Curry

1 cup lentils	6 cups water
1/2 teaspoon turmeric	1 Tablespoon canola oil
1 large onion, diced	2 tomatoes, chopped
3 to 4 cloves garlic, minced	1-1/2 Tablespoon curry powder
2 teaspoons cumin	Salt and pepper to taste
1/4 teaspoon ground cloves	2 cups pumpkin, cubed
2 cups potatoes, cubed	2 medium carrots, diced
2 cups shredded kale,	2 apples, diced unpeeled
2 teaspoons tomato paste	

Cook lentils and turmeric in the water about 45 minutes over medium-low heat. Drain, reserving 2-1/2 cups cooking liquid. Heat oil in a large saucepan; add onion, sauté over medium heat for 4 minutes. Add tomatoes and garlic, cooking 4 minutes more, stirring occasionally. Add curry, cumin, salt, pepper and cloves. Cook another minute, stirring frequently. Stir in lentils, reserved cooking liquid, pumpkin, potatoes, tomato paste and carrots. Cook over medium-low heat until vegetables are tender, approximately 35 to 40 minutes. Stir in greens and apples and cook for 15 minutes more, stirring occasionally. Serve hot.

Mashed Potatoes & Pumpkin

2-1/2 cups pumpkin, cubed	Butter to taste
2-1/2 cups potatoes, cubed	Salt & pepper to taste
1 onion; finely chopped	

Boil peeled potatoes and pumpkin, together. When soft, drain and add onion, and butter. Mash until creamy, season to taste.

Baby Stuffed Pumpkins with Herbs & Bread Crumbs

4 pumpkins, 4 to 5 inch diameter	1/2 cup celery, diced
2 cups rye bread, cubed	1 teaspoon oregano
1/2 cup carrots, sliced	1/2 teaspoon black pepper
1 cup onion, diced	1/4 cup parsley, minced
1/2 cup vegetable broth	1 teaspoon olive oil

Preheat oven to 325 ° F. Cut off pumpkin tops and set aside to use as covers. Scoop out seeds and membranes; set aside for another use. Set pumpkin shells on a large baking sheet, in a medium bowl, combine remaining ingredients and toss well. Pack tightly into pumpkin cavities. Cover with tops. Bake 45 minutes, or until pumpkin shells are tender. Serve hot.

Pumpkin Casserole

1-1/2 lbs pumpkin	2 Tablespoons butter, melted
1 large onion, chopped	2 eggs
1/2 teaspoon salt	3/4 cup milk
1/4 teaspoon pepper	3/4 cup farmers' cheese or ricotta

Preheat oven to 375 ° F. Peel pumpkin and slice the pumpkin into 1/4-inch slices and place in a mixing bowl. Add the onion, salt, pepper and butter and toss well. Pour contents of the bowl into a 9-inch round or square greased baking dish, cover with foil and place in the oven. Bake for 30 minutes.

Meanwhile, beat eggs, milk and cheese together until smooth. Remove the baking dish from the oven. Remove the cover and pour cheese mixture over the top. Return to oven uncovered, another 20 minutes or when topping is golden brown.

Pumpkin & Cauliflower Casserole

1 cup bread crumbs, whole wheat	2 Tablespoons flour
1/2 cup pumpkin seeds	2 cloves garlic, minced
1 Tablespoon butter, melted	2 teaspoons mustard seeds
1 teaspoon dried thyme leaves	1-1/2 teaspoons kosher salt
3/4 cup crumbled goat cheese	1 teaspoon cumin seeds
1 pumpkin, quartered	1/2 teaspoon pepper
1 head cauliflower, quartered	1-1/2 cups half-and-half

Assemble vegetables: Preheat oven to 400° F. Butter a 1-1/2 quart casserole or baking dish and set aside.

Combine bread crumbs, pumpkin seeds (hulled and roasted), butter and half the thyme in a medium bowl, stir in the goat cheese and set aside.

Slice the peeled pumpkin quarters into 1/8-inch-thick pieces and repeat with the cauliflower quarters. Combine flour, garlic, mustard seeds, salt, cumin seeds, pepper and remaining thyme in a small bowl. Spread 1/3 of the pumpkin in the bottom of casserole and sprinkle with 2 teaspoons of the flour mixture. Repeat with 1/2 of the cauliflower and 2 teaspoons of flour. Continue layering with remaining pumpkin, cauliflower and flour, finishing with pumpkin on top. Pour half-and-half over the entire casserole, place on a baking sheet and bake in the center of the oven for 30 minutes.

Bake 30 minutes; sprinkle the bread-crumb mixture over the casserole. Return to the oven and bake until golden brown and bubbly, about 30 minutes. Serve hot.

"Apocolocynposis" means fear
of turning into a pumpkin

Pumpkin Ravioli with Pumpkin Seed Sauce

RAVIOLI
1 cup ricotta cheese
1/2 cup pumpkin, cooked
1/2 teaspoon salt
1/4 teaspoon nutmeg
2 cups flour
1/2 teaspoon salt
1/4 teaspoon tomato paste
1 Tablespoon oil
2 eggs

PUMPKIN SEED SAUCE
1 cup shelled pumpkin seeds
1/2 cup onion
1 slice white bread,
1 clove garlic, crushed
2 Tablespoons oil
2 Tablespoons green chilies
14 oz chicken broth
1/2 cup whipping cream
Salt

Preparation for Ravioli: Mix cheese, pumpkin, salt and nutmeg, then set aside. Mix flour and 1/2 teaspoon salt in a large bowl, making a well in center. Beat tomato paste, oil and eggs until well blended; pour into well. With fork, gradually bring flour mixture into center, until dough forms a ball. If dough is too dry, mix it up to 2 tablespoons water. Knead on lightly floured surface, adding flour if dough is sticky, until smooth and elastic, about 5 minutes. Cover; let rest 5 minutes.

Divide dough into 4 equal parts and cover. Working with one piece of dough at a time, roll into a rectangle, about 12 x 10 inches. Drop pumpkin mixture by 2 level teaspoonfuls onto half of the rectangle about 1, 1/2 inches apart in 2 rows of 4 mounds each. Moisten edges and in between rows of pumpkin mixture with water. Fold the other half over pumpkin mixture, pressing down around mixture. Trim edges with pastry wheel or knife, cutting between rows of filling to make ravioli. Press edges with fork to seal. Repeat! Place ravioli on towel; let stand, turning once, until dry, about 30 minutes. Cook ravioli in 4 quarts boiling salted water until tender, 10 to 15 minutes, drain carefully.

Pumpkin Seed Sauce

Cook pumpkin seeds, onion, bread and garlic in oil, stirring frequently, until bread is golden brown. Stir in chilies. Place mixture in food processor and process until smooth. Stir in broth, whipping cream and salt. Serve with Pumpkin Ravioli.

Cold Pumpkin Soufflé

2 cups heavy cream
1 can, (30 ounces) pumpkin-pie filling
2 envelopes plus 1 teaspoon unflavored gelatin
1/4 cup Bourbon whiskey or 1 Tablespoon vanilla extract

Prepare a 1-1/2-quart soufflé dish or 2 to 3 quart serving bowl tearing off a piece of foil or waxed paper 4 inches longer than the circumference of the dish. Fold in thirds lengthwise. Fit around outside of dish, leaving a 2 inch collar extending above the dish. Fold over lapping ends together and secure with tape or paper clips.

Beat cream in a large bowl with electric mixer just until soft peaks form when beaters are lifted.

Put 1/2 cup pumpkin-pie filling in a small saucepan. Stir in gelatin. Place over low heat and stir 3 to 4 minutes until gelatin is completely dissolved. Remove from heat. Put the remaining pumpkin-pie filling in a large bowl. Stir in hot gelatin mixture, then stir in bourbon and 1/2 cup whipped cream. Fold in remaining whipped cream until blended. Pour into prepared dish. Cover with plastic wrap and refrigerate at least 4 hours. BEFORE SERVING: Remove collar. Spread top of soufflé with whipped cream. Score lightly with knife and sprinkle with cinnamon. Press nuts into sides of soufflé or if serving from a bowl, sprinkle over whipped cream.

Spicy Pumpkin

1 onion, finely sliced
1 garlic clove, crushed
2 teaspoons Curry powder
3 cloves, crushed
1/2 red chili, finely chopped
1 lb. Pumpkin, peeled &
cut in 1 inch cubes

2 tomatoes, chopped
1 Tablespoon golden raisins
1/4 teaspoon sugar, optional
1 lemon, juice of
2 Tablespoons Oil
Salt and pepper

Heat oil in a heavy pan adding onion, sauté until onion is transparent. Add garlic, continuing to cook. Next put in curry powder, ground cloves, chopped tomatoes, sultanas and sugar. Sprinkle the lemon juice over the mixture, and. cover, cooking gently for 30 to 40 minutes or until pumpkin is tender. Stir frequently; season and serve to accompany main dishes and rice.

Grilled Pumpkin

6-1/2 Tablespoons butter; softened
1 teaspoon herbs, mixed
Salt and pepper to taste

2-1/4 lbs pumpkin
Fresh lemon juice

Preheat the oven to 350° F. Peel and clean pumpkin and cut into slivers. Combine butter and herbs and season to taste. Arrange the pumpkin slivers on a baking tray, spread with a little herb butter, and bake for about 30 minutes, or until tender, basting the pumpkins with the butter as needed during baking. When ready to serve, season to taste and sprinkle with lemon juice. This dish is good served with fish.

Pumpkin Vegetable Dish

3 Tablespoons butter
2-1/4 lbs pumpkin, fresh
1/2 cup meat stock
Salt and pepper to taste

Sugar, to taste
Vinegar, to taste
2 Tablespoons dill, chopped
2 Tablespoons parsley, chopped

Peel and clean pumpkin and cut into sticks. In a large skillet, melt the butter, and braise the pumpkin sticks. Add meat stock, bring to a boil and simmer for about 8 minutes, or until tender. Season to taste. Stir in dill and parsley. Serve immediately.

Pumpkin & "Peas"

1 Tablespoon butter
1/2 cup onion, finely chopped
1 cup lentils
3 cups water
1 pinch cumin, ground
1/3 cup scallion tops, sliced

1/2 teaspoon ginger, ground
1/4 teaspoon salt
1/8 teaspoon black pepper
3 cups pumpkin,
1 Tablespoon lemon juice
1 Tablespoon parsley, minced

In a large saucepan, melt butter, then, sauté the onion until soft. Stir in lentils and pour in the water (enough to cover lentils). Bring to a boil. Reduce heat and simmer, covered. Stir occasionally for 20 minutes. Add the pumpkin, lemon juice, parsley, ginger, salt, pepper and cumin, stirring to combine. Cover and cook an additional 15 minutes or until the pumpkin is tender. Toss with the scallion tops just before serving.

Rice with Pumpkin Italian Style

1-1/4 cups rice	1/3 cup butter
4-1/4 cups vegetable broth	1 mall onion, chopped
1-1/2 lbs pumpkin	Salt and pepper to taste
4 Tablespoons olive oil	

In a large pan, heat 1/2 the oil, 1/2 the butter, add salt, pepper and pumpkin, cubed; cooking until tender. A small amount of water may be added if necessary. Bring broth to a simmer and adjust heat to keep it hot but not boiling.

In a large saucepan, sauté onion with the remaining oil and butter, then add rice and stir for a couple of minutes. Add the pumpkin and 1 cup of the hot broth; stir, add another as needed to keep rice from drying out, stirring to keep it from sticking. Only add more liquid whenever rice starts sticking or looking dry. When the rice is done, add more butter and serve hot.

Spicy Stewed Pumpkin

1 cup water	4 cloves
1/4 cup vinegar	Non cal sweetener to taste
1 small cinnamon stock	4 cups Pumpkin, cubed
1 small piece fresh ginger	

In a saucepan, combine ingredients except pumpkin and boil for a few minutes. Peel, seed and cube the pumpkin. Drop the pumpkin cubes into the saucepan with spices. Cook gently until tender, stirring frequently. Divide into 4 equal servings. Serve warm or cold.

In colonial times, Native Americans roasted long strips of pumpkin in an open fire.

Pumpkin Walnut Loaf

1 cup onion, minced
1/2 cup bell pepper, minced
1 cup pumpkin, diced
1/4 cup chicken broth
1 cup cooked long-grain rice
6 Tablespoons bread crumbs
2 oz. walnuts, finely chopped
2 Tablespoons butter or oil

1 egg, beaten
2 Tablespoons parsley, minced
3/4 teaspoon salt
1/2 teaspoon sage
1/4 teaspoon pepper
3/4 oz. parmesan cheese
1-1/2 cup stewed tomatoes

Preheat oven to 375° F. Melt butter in a large skillet, stir in onion and bell pepper, cook over medium heat, stirring often, until onion is pale gold, about 5 minutes. Add pumpkin and broth, cover and cook over low heat until pumpkin is soft, about 7 minutes. Remove from heat, add rice, breadcrumbs, walnuts, egg, parsley, salt, sage, and pepper; mix well.

Spray a 4-cup baking dish with nonstick cooking spray. Pack rice mixture into dish. Sprinkle with freshly grated Parmesan, and bake 25 minutes. Broil for 1 or 2 minutes until lightly browned on top.
Meanwhile, in a small saucepan, bring the stewed tomatoes to a boil over high heat, stirring frequently. Cook uncovered until reduced to 1 cup. Puree in blender or food processor. Serve loaf with sauce on the side.

Curried Pumpkin

1 lb pumpkin
1/3 onion
2 fresh chilies
4 cloves garlic
2 Tablespoons olive oil
a sprig curry leaves
1 teaspoon salt
1/2 teaspoon lime juice

1/4 teaspoon black pepper
1/4 teaspoon turmeric
3 cups thin coconut milk
1/2 cup thick coconut milk
2 Tablespoons ground rice
1 teaspoon ground mustard
pinch curry powder

Cut top off of pumpkin. After cleaning, scoop out flesh and cube. Set shell aside. Slice onion, chili, and crush garlic. Heat oil and sauté onion, chili and curry together. When the onion is soft, add pumpkin, salt, pepper, turmeric and thin coconut milk; cook until the pumpkin is tender. Pour the thick coconut milk onto the ground rice, add mustard and add to the pumpkin mixture, stirring as it thickens. Bring to a boil and simmer a few minutes. Remove from heat and spoon into pumpkin shell. Sprinkle with the curry powder and lime juice.

Pumpkin Fettuccini

1 cup canned pumpkin
1 cup cream
1 cup grated parmesan cheese
Salt and pepper

1/2 teaspoon grated nutmeg
1/4 cup butter
12 oz fettuccini, cooked

Mix pumpkin, cream, 1/2 cup cheese and nutmeg in a small saucepan. Simmer over low heat. Add butter to fettuccini in large bowl and toss to melt butter. Pour pumpkin mixture over pasta. Sprinkle with remaining cheese.

A Pilgrim described the hardships of the New Word as follows (1630): "For pottage and puddings and custard and pies, our pumpkins and parsnip are common supplies: we have pumpkins at morning and pumpkins at noon, if it were not for pumpkins, we should be undoon"

Pumpkin -n- Pasta

1 small pumpkin, cubed	1 teaspoon nutmeg
4 shallots, diced	Black pepper
18 oz. very dry hard cider	1 cup grated parmesan cheese
3 Tablespoons butter	1 lb orecchiete or penne

Sauté shallots in olive oil until soft, and then add pumpkin; cooking about 5 minutes, add the cider, butter, nutmeg, and pepper. Bring to a boil and simmer until the pumpkin is very soft. Add more cider if the sauce starts getting too thick. Mash sauce in the pot with a potato masher or puree in a food processor. Cook and drain pasta and return it to the cooking pot. Pour in most of the sauce, except one cup. Add Parmesan; and stir well.

Stewed Pumpkin

1 lb. pumpkin, cubed	1 clove garlic, minced
2 Tablespoons cooking oil	2 scallions, minced
Salt and pepper to taste	

Place pumpkin, butter, garlic and scallions in a saucepan. Cook over medium heat, stirring, until the butter melts. Reduce heat and cover, cooking until the pumpkin is tender. Stir mixture occasionally to prevent sticking. Season and cook 3 minutes.

Fried Pumpkin

1 medium size pumpkin	Sorghum molasses
Enough oil to grease skillet for frying	Salt

Cut and slice pumpkin, cleaning out seed. Scrape inside clean and quarter pumpkin. Bake until its soft enough to spoon out of shell. Put in a greased, hot iron skillet ready for flying. Add salt to taste if desired. When pumpkin begins to get soft to a fork test, add as much sorghum molasses to taste, to sweeten. Continue to cook until pumpkin turns orange brown in color. Stir often to keep from scorching.

Soups
&
Chowder

Pumpkin Soup Tureen

Preparing the pumpkin shell

1. Select a squat pumpkin rather than one that is upright for balance. Look for one that has the ideal bowl shape.

2. Wash pumpkin in warm soapy water rinse well and dry.

3. Cut away the top to form a lid. Scoop out the seeds and stringy mass.

4. Lightly oil pumpkin inside and out and sprinkle the inside with salt.

5. Place pumpkin and lid on a parchment lined baking sheet or spray with a oil cooking spray. Bake at 325 ° F, just long enough for it to begin to soften. Over baking the shell makes it unable to support the weight of the soup. Under-baking is preferred.

6. Remove from the oven and cool.

7. Gently scoop out some of the soft pumpkin from the wall, being careful not to puncture the shell. Scrape the cooked pumpkin from the lid as well. Use this cooked portion for any pumpkin soup recipe or freeze it for later use.

8. Pour hot soup into the pumpkin shell and serve. The lid can be used as a cover or you can serve the soup uncovered.

Quick & Easy Creamy Pumpkin Soup

2 cups finely chopped onions	1-1/2 teaspoons ground cumin
2 green onions, sliced	1 bay leaf
1/2 cup finely chopped celery	1 cup evaporated skim milk
1 green chili pepper, chopped	Salt and pepper to taste
1/2 cup canola or vegetable oil	Parmesan cheese
3 cans chicken broth	Fresh parsley, chopped
2 cups pumpkin puree	

In a 6-quart saucepan, sauté onions, green onions, celery and chili pepper in oil. Cook until onions begin to look translucent. Add broth, pumpkin, bay leaf, and cumin. Bring to a boil. Reduce heat and simmer, uncovered for 20 minutes, stirring occasionally. Remove bay leaf. Add evaporated milk and cook over low heat for 5 minutes. Do not boil. Taste to adjust seasoning, if necessary. Add 1/2 teaspoon salt and 1/2 teaspoon black pepper, if desired. Transfer hot soup to pumpkin tureen. Garnish with grated Parmesan cheese and chopped parsley. Serve hot. Makes 6 to 8 servings.

Fresh Corn & Pumpkin Soup

3 ears of corn,	1 yellow onion, peeled and sliced
10 oz frozen corn	1 cup water
1 2-1/2 to 3 lbs. pumpkin	Salt and pepper to taste

Shell the corn from the cob. In a food processor, puree fresh and frozen corn together, just enough to mash. Peel and seed the pumpkin and cut into small pieces. Place all ingredients in a covered saucepan and simmer until the pumpkin is soft, about 30 minutes. Serve hot.

Pumpkin Soup with Gruyere Cheese

STOCK:

Pumpkin center seeds and scrapings
2 carrots, peeled and diced
1 celery stock, chopped
1 turnip, peeled and diced
2 bay leaves

1/2 teaspoon dried sage
4 parsley branches
3 thyme branches
1/2 teaspoon salt
8 cups cold water

Use pumpkins that are not very stringy for best results. Cut in half and scrape out all the seeds and stringy material and put into a pot with remaining ingredients, bring to a boil, simmer for 25 minutes, and then strain. Use pumpkin halves for soup.

SOUP:

2 pumpkin halves
3 Tablespoons butter
1 yellow onion diced
1/2 teaspoon salt
Thyme leaves for garnish

6 to 7 cups stock
1/2 to 1 cup light cream
White pepper
3 oz Gruyere cheese, finely grated

Preheat oven to 400° F. Bake the pumpkin halves, skin up, on a lightly oiled baking sheet until the skin is wrinkled and the flesh is soft, about one hour. Remove pumpkin from the oven, and when cool enough to handle, peel off the skin. Reserve any caramelized juices that collect in the pan. Melt butter in a soup pot, add the onion, and cook over medium heat for about 5 minutes. Add the cooked pumpkin, juices left in pan, salt and about 6 cups stock. Bring to a boil; then cover and simmer for 25 minutes.

Pass the soup through a food mill, smoothing it out but leaving some texture. Return the soup to pot adding cream and more stock, to desired consistency. Add seasonings to taste.. Stir in grated cheese and serve with thyme leave scattered lightly over soup.

Pumpkin-Mushroom Bisque

1 16-ounce can of pumpkin
1/4 teaspoon pepper
1 Tablespoon margarine or butter
Sliced green onions
1 cup thinly sliced fresh mushrooms
1 12-ounce can evaporated skim milk
3/4 cup frozen orange juice concentrate, thawed
2-1/2 cups reduced-sodium or regular chicken broth

1/2 cup chopped onion
Dash of ground cinnamon
1/8 teaspoon salt
Roasted pumpkin seeds

In a large saucepan cook mushrooms and onion in margarine until tender. Add broth, pumpkin, milk, pepper, salt, and cinnamon. Heat through but do not boil. Stir in thawed concentrate; heat but do not boil. Garnish with green onion.

Cream of Pumpkin Soup

1 large onion
1/4 cup butter
1 16 oz. can pumpkin
4 cups chicken broth
1 bay leaf
1/2 teaspoon sugar

1/2 teaspoon curry powder
1/8 teaspoon nutmeg
1 Tablespoon dry parsley
2 cups half and half
2 teaspoons salt
Ground pepper to taste

Quarter onion and slice thinly, then sauté in butter till golden. Stir in chicken broth, bay leaf, sugar, curry, nutmeg and parsley. Bring to boil and simmer uncovered 15 minutes, stirring occasionally. Add half and half in a thin stream, stirring while adding. Add salt and pepper. Simmer 5-10 minutes.

Pumpkin Tomato Chowder

2 Tablespoons butter
1/4 cup bell pepper, chopped
2 Tablespoons onion, chopped
1 large sprig parsley, chopped
1/8 teaspoon dried thyme leaves
1 cup canned tomatoes
1 can pumpkin

1/8 teaspoon pepper
1 bay leaf
1 teaspoon salt
1 Tablespoon flour
2 cups chicken stock
1 cup half and half

Melt butter and add green pepper, onion, parsley, thyme and bay leaf. Cook five minutes. Add tomatoes, pumpkin, and chicken stock. Cover and simmer 30 minutes, stirring occasionally. Puree in blender or food processor. Blend together, flour and half and half, and stir into soup. Add salt and pepper and cook at medium or medium low temperature, stirring frequently, until thickens. Serve hot or cold.

Pumpkin & White Bean Soup

2 Tablespoons vegetable oil
1 medium onion, diced
1 cup diced celery
2 cloves garlic, minced
1 jalapeno pepper
1 Tablespoon minced ginger
4 cups peeled, diced pumpkin
2 Tablespoons minced parsley
1-1/2 cups cooked navy beans, drained

1 Tablespoon thyme
1 Tablespoon curry powder
1 teaspoon ground cumin
1/2 teaspoon salt
1/2 teaspoon ground allspice
6 cups water
1 cup kale or spinach

Heat oil in a large sauce-pan, add onion, celery, garlic, chili pepper, and ginger. Sauté over medium heat for 7 minutes, then add pumpkin and sauté for 3 minutes. Add seasonings and continue to sauté for 1 minute longer. Add water and simmer for about 20 minutes, stirring occasionally. Stir in the kale and white beans and cook for another 10 to 15 minutes.

Cheese Soup in a Pumpkin Shell

1 medium size pumpkin	1/4 teaspoon salt
2 Tablespoons butter, melted	1/4 teaspoon pepper
2 Tablespoons butter	1/4 teaspoon nutmeg
1 large onion, chopped	3/4 cup light cream
2 large carrots, shredded	1 cup cheddar or
2 celery slicks, chopped	Gruyere cheese, grated
4 cups vegetable broth	1/3 cup dry white wine
1 garlic clove, minced	2 Tablespoons parsley, minced

Preheat oven to 350° F. Butter a baking sheet.

Prepare pumpkin:
Cut off the top, scoop out seeds, brush inside with 2 tablespoons melted butter. Replace top and place pumpkin on a baking sheet. Bake 45 minutes or until tender when pierced with a fork. The pumpkin should be a bit droopy but still hold its shape well.

Meanwhile, melt 2 tablespoons butter in a large saucepan. Add onion, carrots, celery. Sauté until soft; about 10 minutes, add broth, garlic, salt, pepper, and nutmeg. Cover, and simmer 20 minutes. Cool slightly.
Puree vegetable mixture in food processor then return it to the saucepan; stir in the cream and re-heat. Add cheese and wine, heat until cheese melts. Stir frequently after adding milk to avoid scorching. Do not allow soup come to a boil. Place hot pumpkin on serving platter. Pour in soup. Sprinkle with parsley.

Notes:
Serve the soup by ladling out of the pumpkin at the table, scooping a little bit of pumpkin into each serving. The pumpkin makes a great presentation.

Simple Potato Pumpkin Soup

4 Tablespoons butter
Vegetable stock to cover ingredients
3 lbs. pumpkin cubed

2 lbs. potatoes
2 yellow onions
2 cups heavy cream

Quarter onions and sauté them gently in butter in the base of a large pan until just soft. Add 3 pounds of pumpkin, cubed, and 2 pounds of potatoes. Cover with vegetable stock and simmer until everything is very tender. Use electric mixer or food processor to bring to a creamy consistency. Add 2 cups heavy cream. Season with salt, pepper, garlic powder and liquid smoke to taste as desired. Freezes well.

Pumpkin & Broccoli Chowder

1 Tablespoon maple syrup or honey
1 large onion, chopped
1 Tablespoon soy sauce
1 ripe tomato, diced
4 cups chicken stock
1/2 cup heavy (whipping) cream

4 Tablespoons butter
Salt to taste
Ground black pepper-to taste
1 bunch broccoli, flowerets
Broccoli stems, cut in strips
4 cups pumpkin puree

In a 10 inch skillet, melt the butter over medium-low heat. Add the onion and sauté slowly until almost limp but not brown, about 6 to 7 minutes. Add the soy sauce and the tomato. Cook stirring often, until the tomato's juice has evaporated, about 6 minutes. Transfer the sautéed mixture to a soup pot. Deglaze the sauté pan with 1 cup of the stock and pour into the soup pot contents, plus the remaining 3 cups of the stock. Add the pumpkin puree, the maple syrup or honey, salt and a touch of freshly ground black pepper. Heat; stir often. Separately, in a small pot with a tightly fitting lid, steam the broccoli flowerets and stems until tender-crisp (they should be a bright green), about 3 to 4 minutes. Stir the steamed broccoli into the soup then stir in the cream. Let the soup cook over low heat, stirring occasionally, until hot and the flavors have blended, 8-10 minutes.

Apple Pumpkin Soup with Ginger

12 cups of diced pumpkin
3 medium sized apples
4 cups chicken stock

3 Tablespoons. butter
1 cup of heavy cream
Salt, ginger, chives

Boil the diced pumpkin until tender. Peel apples, quarter and remove the core. Boil apples until tender. Set aside.

In a food processor, puree pumpkin. Add some chicken stock to make the blending easier. Add the apples until smooth consistency. Add the remaining chicken stock, cup of heavy cream, and 3 tablespoons of butter. You may have to do this process in separate steps. The important thing is that all components are thoroughly mix, having a nice looking puree consistency. Strain and salt to taste.

Take 1/2 cup of the soup and 1 to 2 inch piece of fresh peeled ginger and liquefy. Strain this mixture in a fine mesh and add slowly until you reach your preferred taste for ginger. Garnish; sprinkling thinly with cut chives.

Easy Pumpkin Soup

4 cups chicken broth
1 onion, chopped
2 cups pumpkin
3/4 cup green onions,
2 cups milk

1/8 teaspoon nutmeg
1/2 teaspoon curry powder
1/2 teaspoon sugar
Chopped bay leaf
Salt and pepper to taste

Sauté onions and add other ingredients and cook uncovered 15 minutes. Puree then add milk and cook another 5 minutes. Do not boil.

Potato Pumpkin Rutabaga Soup with Rice

2 pounds pumpkin	Salt
2 large potatoes	Ground white pepper
1 large onion	1 or 2 stock cubes
2 medium tomatoes	2 oz butter
1 rutabaga	Several sprigs fresh rosemary
2 carrots	Cooked rice
3 pints cold water	

Peel the pumpkin, carrots, rutabaga, and potatoes and cut into cubes. Cut tomatoes in half and remove the seeds (leave skin on). Chop the onion. Put all the vegetables into a pot containing the water. Bring to a boil; then, season with salt, pepper, stock cubes and rosemary. Stir and taste; correct seasonings. Cover and simmer until tender. Turn off heat, add butter and allow to a cool with lid on. When cool; stir in butter. Blend in a blender, to a smooth, thick consistency. To serve: re-heat soup until piping hot. Add cooked rice and serve.

To store:
To store, keep in the refrigerator in a sealed container for up to 4 days, or freeze in a well sealed container and store for up to 6 months.

Pumpkin Soup

1 2-1/2 lbs. Pumpkin
2 teaspoon instant chicken stock
2 teaspoons green herbs stock
2 cloves garlic, chopped
2 to 3 cups milk

2 cups water
2 onions, chopped
2 teaspoons sugar
1/4 teaspoon grated Nutmeg

Remove seeds and stringy parts from pumpkin. Do not remove skin. Cut into chunks. Put pieces, skin side down, with all the ingredients (except the milk) in a large pot. Cover and cook gently until pumpkin is tender enough to scrape the pulp from its skin. Puree pulp with onion and cooking liquid in batches, using a food processor, or sieve. Add 2 cups milk to the puree. Re-heat without boiling adding more milk if soup is too thick. Top each serving with a spoonful of whipped cream or fresh chopped herbs. Serves 6 to 8.

Pumpkin-Millet Soup

1 small or medium small pumpkin (about 1-1/2 lbs.)
6 cups broth (vegetable or chicken)
1 cup dry millet
1 to 2 teaspoon nutmeg
1/8 teaspoon cayenne pepper

Bring the broth to a boil in a large stockpot, add millet, and simmer for about 30 min, until millet is well cooked. Peel and clean pumpkin, cutting meat into cubes and add to broth when millet is done. Mix, and simmer for another 15 to 20 min, until squash is tender. Puree the mixture in a processor until it is reduced to a creamy texture. Add the nutmeg and pepper, and re-heat. Serve with a scoop of plain yogurt in each bowl.

Pumpkins are members of the vine crops family called cucurbits.

Pumpkin Apple Soup

STOCK (SOUP)

Seeds and strings from the pumpkin
3 crisp, apples quartered
(Granny Smith, Wine sap, etc.)
3 cups pumpkin puree
1 head garlic
1 large onion, quartered
1-1/2 teaspoon salt
1 Tablespoon curry powder

1/2 cup apple juice concentrate
1 apple, washed, cored and diced
1 large onion, diced
3 Tablespoons olive oil
5 cups soup stock
Zest of 1/2 orange
6 cups water

GARNISH

Paprika
1 cup half and half

3 cups pumpkin puree

Stock:

Place all ingredients in a large pot, bring to a boil, turn heat down and simmer covered for 45 minutes. Let the stock cool for about 30 minutes, strain and discard solids. Measure 5 cups stock; if it is less, add water, if it is more use it.

Soup:

Sauté onions in olive oil for about 3 minutes. Add the diced apple and sauté for 2 minutes longer. Sprinkle with curry powder and sauté one minute longer. Remove from heat and set aside. Using half the onions and apples, sauté in a large pot. Add the stock made ahead of time, along with pumpkin puree. Bring this mixture to a boil; reduce temperature and simmer gently for about 10 minutes. Stir occasionally. Meanwhile put the other half of the apples and onions sauté and the apple juice concentrate in a food processor or blender. Process until smooth; add to the soup pot. Add evaporated milk and continue cooking until the soup is very hot. Do not allow soup to come to a boil again. Serve the soup garnished with a spoonful of the apple/onion sauté and a dash of paprika.

Kumara, Pumpkin & Peanut Soup

1 large onion
1 teaspoon finely chopped garlic
2 Tablespoons butter or oil
1/2 teaspoon curry powder
1/2 teaspoon ground coriander
1/8 to 1/4 teaspoon chili powder

1-1/2 lbs. sweet potato
1/2 lb. Pumpkin
4 cups chicken stock
1/2 teaspoon salt
2 Tablespoons peanut butter

Cook the chopped onion and garlic over low heat in butter or oil, in a medium sized saucepan until the onion is transparent. Add the curry powder, coriander and chili powder to taste, to the onion mixture and stir over a moderate heat for about 1 minute. Chop the peeled sweet potato and pumpkin into small cubes. Add vegetables to the stock, bring to a boil and simmer for about 15 minutes or until the vegetables are tender. Add salt first, then the peanut butter, stirring until peanut butter has melted and is mixed in. Puree soup in a food processor or mash well with a potato masher. Adjust seasonings and re-heat. Serve topped with a swirl of yogurt, coconut cream or plain cream.

Fresh Pumpkin Soup

1 Tablespoon butter
1 small onion, chopped fine
1 lb, fresh pumpkin, pureed
2 cups chicken stock
1/2 teaspoon thyme

1 bay leaf
1 cup cream
1/4 cup dry sherry
Chopped chives to garnish

Melt butter in soup pan. Sauté onion in butter until golden in color, stir in: pumpkin, chicken stock, thyme and bay leaf. Cook over low heat 15 minutes, stirring occasionally, until mixture is smooth. Remove from heat, and cool. Stir in cream and sherry, and heat thoroughly. Remove bay leaf. Garnish with chopped chives.

Black Bean Pumpkin Soup

1/2 stick unsalted butter
1-1/4 cups chopped onion
1/2 cup minced shallot
1/2 cup dry sherry
1/2 lb. turkey ham, shredded
3 to 4 Tablespoons sherry vinegar
3 cans black beans, rinsed & drained
1 cup drained canned tomatoes, chopped
1 Tablespoon + 2 teaspoons ground cumin

4 garlic cloves, minced
4 cups beef broth
16-oz can pumpkin puree
1 teaspoon salt
1/2 teaspoon ground pepper

GARNISH
Sour cream and lightly toasted pumpkin seeds

Coarsely puree beans and tomatoes in a food processor, set aside. Sauté onions and shallots with cumin, salt and pepper, in butter over medium heat, stir until onions are softened and begin to brown. Stir in bean puree. Stir in broth, sherry and pumpkin, until combined and simmer, uncovered, stirring occasionally, for 25 minutes. Just before serving add turkey ham and vinegar, stir until heated through. Season soup with salt and pepper. Garnish with a dollop of sour cream and toasted pumpkin seeds. Makes about 9 cups.

Lentil Pumpkin Soup

1/2 pumpkin peeled and chopped
1 onion chopped
1 Tablespoon extra virgin olive oil
1 teaspoon Coriander
1 teaspoon ground cumin
Ground black pepper

Cayenne pepper to taste
2 cloves garlic chopped
1/2 inch ginger chopped
1 cup red lentils
2/3 cup tomato puree
Sour cream

Sauté onion, garlic and ginger and spices in oil, until onion is soft. Add pumpkin and lentils and cover with water. Simmer for 20 minutes, occasionally adding water if needed. The soup will become quite thick. Mash mixture with a potato masher. Add tomato paste and simmer for another five minutes. Serve topped with sour cream and black pepper.

Mushroom Pumpkin Soup

2 to 3 lbs. Mushrooms
2 Tablespoons olive oil
2 cloves garlic minced
2 large cans cooked pumpkin (56 oz. total)
Salt, pepper, poultry season and nutmeg

1/2 cup dry sherry wine
1 to 2 quarts chicken stock
1 bay leaf

Sauté sliced mushrooms in a few tablespoons of oil in a large skillet until soft and tender. Splash in some crushed garlic and sherry (1/2 cup or to taste) bay leaf and cook mushrooms on low heat until most of liquid has evaporated , but mushrooms are still moist.

Place pumpkin in a large pot; thin with chicken stock to desired consistency and heat gently, stirring in the mushrooms. Continue to simmer about 1/2 hour to blend flavors. Season with salt, pepper, bit of fresh grated nutmeg and poultry seasoning to taste. Best when made the day before you want to serve.

Spicy Pumpkin Soup

1 teaspoon finely chopped garlic
2 teaspoon ground cumin
1 teaspoon ground coriander seeds
1-1/2 lbs. pumpkin
1 teaspoon Tabasco sauce

1 Tablespoon oil
1 cup water
1/2 teaspoon salt
1 cup coconut cream

In a medium-sized pot, gently cook the garlic in the oil about a minute; add the ground cumin and the crushed coriander seeds. Heat for another minute or two, until the spices are aromatic but have not darkened too much. Add the pumpkin, cut in small cubes, then cover and cook gently in the water for 10 minutes or until tender. Puree the pumpkin, spices, and cooking liquid in a food processor, or blender, then, add coconut cream, salt and Tabasco sauce in quantities to suit your taste.

Autumn Pumpkin Bisque

1 large pumpkin	1/8 cup brown sugar
4 vegetable bouillon cubes	1/2 teaspoon allspice
3 cups heavy cream	1/2 teaspoon cinnamon
1/2 cup butter	1/2 teaspoon nutmeg
1/2 cup Brandy	1/2 teaspoon pepper
2 bottles beer, (quality malt liqueur)	1 to 2 Tablespoons salt

In a large pot, bring 1-1/2 gallons of water and 1 tablespoon salt to a boil. Peel, seed and cut pumpkin into large chunks then add to boiling water and boil until tender. Strain Pumpkin from liquid, returning the remaining liquid to the stove and reduce until only 2-1/2 cups remain. In a sauce pan, place beer, brandy, brown sugar, and shallots. Bring to a boil, boiling this mixture until reduced by 1/2; set aside.

Divide pumpkin, putting 1/2 into an oven at 350° to remove some of the moisture; about 15 minutes. Place the other half in a food processor and puree to a creamy paste using some of the stock to thin if necessary. Set aside.

When pumpkin stock is reduced, add pumpkin puree and cinnamon. Remove pumpkin chunks from oven, dice into small bits and add to stock. Add allspice, nutmeg, black pepper and salt to taste. Place soup over a double boiler, on stove and add butter and cream, whisk soup to blend together. Cook 30 minutes and serve.

Spiced Pumpkin & Coconut Soup

1 Tablespoon butter
4 cloves garlic
2 teaspoons ground cumin
1 teaspoon ground coriander
1 teaspoon pepper sauce, or to taste

1-1/2 lbs. Pumpkin
1 cup water
1 cup coconut cream
1/2 teaspoon salt

Cook butter and finely chopped garlic together in a large pan with lid on, for several minutes, being careful not to burn the garlic. Add the spices and cook a little longer before adding the pieces of uncooked pumpkin and water. Cover and cook gently for until pumpkin is tender, adding more water as it evaporates during cooking. Let sit until cool enough to handle, then scoop out the seeds and peel skin, discarding them. Puree in a food processor then add coconut cream, salt and hot pepper sauce. Taste to balance the flavors, adding more water or coconut cream if you wish. Sieve the soup to remove any debris, then re-heat and serve.

Pumpkin Peanut Butter Soup

1-1/2 lbs. yams
6 Tablespoons butter
2 Tablespoons shallots
4 cups solid pack pumpkin
8 cups chicken broth
Snipped fresh chives

1 cup unsalted peanut butter
2 teaspoons mustard
1/2 teaspoon grated nutmeg
Salt and ground pepper
Chopped roasted unsalted peanuts

Preheat oven to 350° F. Place yams on baking sheet and bake until knife pierces centers easily, about 1 hour. Cool yams; peel. Puree in processor. Melt butter in a large heavy pot over medium heat. Mince shallots and add to pot; sauté 2 minutes. Mix in 2 cups yam puree and pumpkin. Pour broth and add peanut butter alternately, stirring until smooth. Simmer until thickened, stirring occasionally; about 25 minutes. Stir in mustard and nutmeg. Season with salt and pepper! Garnish with nuts and chives.

Pumpkin-Tomato Cream Soup

2 cups chopped onion
1 garlic clove
3 Tablespoons clarified butter
2 cups chicken broth
1 teaspoon salt
1/2 teaspoon grated nutmeg
1/2 teaspoon ground allspice

1/2 teaspoon ground coriander
1/8 teaspoon ground pepper
1/4 teaspoon cayenne pepper
2 cups light cream
2 cups canned pumpkin
2 Tablespoons tomato paste
1 (15 oz) can diced tomatoes, drained

Cook onions in clarified butter, covered over a moderately low, to low heat for 15 minutes. Add the garlic clove to the pan, continuing to cook onions and garlic for 10 to 15 minutes longer. Onions will be done when onions are a light golden color and most of the moisture has evaporated.

Divide onions in half. Using some of the chicken broth, blend half the onions in a blender until onions are pureed. Combine remaining chicken broth, pureed onions, cooked diced onions, spices, and garlic in a large, covered saucepan. Bring mixture to a boil. Reduce heat and simmer, covered, for 20 minutes.

Combine light cream and pumpkin together and stir into the saucepan. Add tomato paste and diced tomatoes. Simmer covered for additional 30 minutes, being careful to not let soup boil.

Pumpkin & Leek Soup

1 small pumpkin, cut into pieces
1/2 cup butter
Salt and white pepper
Pinch cayenne pepper
1 cup heavy cream
1 Tablespoon fresh mint, finely chopped
2 leeks, white part only, thinly sliced

2 cups chicken stock
1/3 cup orzo or risoni
1 large onion, chopped
3 or 4 potatoes, peeled and diced
2 cups milk

Preheat oven to 375° F. Place pumpkin pieces skin side up in a large baking dish. Pour over 1/2 cup water and bake for about 1 hour, or until a fork pierces the flesh easily. Melt half of the butter and gently sauté leeks until softened. Remove and set aside. Add remaining butter and cook onion and potatoes until golden. Stir in milk and simmer for 20 minutes.

When pumpkin is tender and golden, remove from oven. Cool; then remove skin and any excessively browned surfaces, in the meantime, put chicken stock on to boil, add orzo and cook until barely done. Remove pasta with a slotted spoon and set aside with leeks. Reserve stock. Blend pumpkin and potato mixture in a food processor or force it through a fine sieve. Season with: salt, pepper, and cayenne to taste. Transfer to a clean saucepan and blend in the hot stock. Add cream, bring to a boil, and then stir in leeks and pasta. If the soup is too thick, thin it with extra stock or water. Adjust the seasoning and stir in mint.

Pumpkin-Peanut Soup

4 cups pumpkin puree	1/4 teaspoon pepper
1/4 cup butter	1 cup chopped onion
1/2 cup diced red pepper	1 large jalapeno pepper
4 cups vegetable broth	1/4 cup peanut butter
1/2 cup heavy cream	1 Tablespoon lime juice
1 teaspoon salt	Thinly sliced scallions

Preheat oven to 350° F. Line jellyroll pan with foil, cut pumpkin in half lengthwise and remove seeds. Sprinkle inside with salt and pepper. Place cut side down on prepared pan. Bake 1 hour or until soft. Set a side until cool enough to handle; then scoop flesh into bowl.

In a heavy pot, melt butter over medium heat; add onion. Sauté 15 minutes, or until golden brown. Add pumpkin, red pepper, jalapeno (seeded, peeled, and minced), and vegetable broth. Bring to a boil. Cover, reduce heat and simmer. Cook 10 minutes, stirring to break up pumpkin.

Remove all but 2 cups soup solids, in a food processor, puree solids and return to soup in pan. Add peanut butter and heavy cream. Over low heat, cook stirring until peanut butter melts. Add limejuice and remaining salt and pepper. Serve sprinkled with scallions. Makes 8 servings.

Pumpkins were once recommended for removing freckles and curing snake bites.

Bread, Muffins, Cookies & Cakes

Buttermilk Pumpkin Muffins

2 cups flour
2 cups yellow corn meal
2 Tablespoons baking powder
1 teaspoon baking soda
2 teaspoon salt
3 eggs

1 cup pumpkin puree
1/2 cup honey
1/2 cup light molasses
2 cups buttermilk
1/4 lb butter, melted

Preheat oven to 425° F. Sift dry ingredients together. Beat eggs thoroughly then add pumpkin, honey, molasses, and buttermilk. Combine with dry ingredients and mix well. Stir in butter. Grease muffin tins and fill 2/3 full with batter. Bake for 20 min., or until golden brown. Cool on wire rack. Makes: 2-1/2 dozen.

Cinnamon Sugar Pumpkin Muffins

2 cup flour
1 teaspoon salt
4 teaspoon baking powder
1/2 cup white sugar
1 teaspoon cinnamon
1 teaspoon allspice
1 teaspoon nutmeg
2 eggs, beaten
1/2 cup vegetable oil

1 teaspoon vanilla
3/4 cup canned pumpkin
1/4 cup molasses
1/8 cup honey
1/8 cup heavy cream
1/2 cup apple cider
1/2 cup milk
1/2 cup raisins
Cinnamon sugar mixture

Sift together flour, salt, baking powder. Add sugar, cinnamon, allspice and nutmeg. Mix well, in another bowl combine eggs, oil, vanilla, pumpkin, molasses, honey, cream, cider and milk. Mix well and add to dry mixture. Mix just until moistened. Add raisins. Spray muffins tin with oil spray. Fill this 3/4 full or more. Sprinkle muffins with cinnamon sugar before baking. Bake 20 minutes at 425° or until knife inserted comes out clean.

Low Fat Pumpkin Ginger Muffins

1 small pumpkin	2 teaspoons ginger
2-1/2 cups cake flour	1/2 cups brown sugar
4 teaspoons baking powder	1/2 cups egg substitute
1 teaspoon baking soda	1/2 cups evaporated milk
1-1/2 cups unsweetened apple sauce	

Bake whole pumpkin at 350° F for one hour or until tender. Remove, and let cool. Peel the cooled pumpkin, and scrape the seeds and fiber out of the center. Mash the remaining pumpkin. You will need 1-1/2 cups.

Preheat oven to 350° F. Mix all of the dry ingredients together. In a separate bowl, combine the moist ingredients, mixing thoroughly. Add the wet ingredients to the dry ones, folding gently. Fold as little as possible until just combined. Fill twelve muffin cups with the batter until almost foil (either spray with nonstick cooking spray or use paper muffin cups). Bake for 25 minutes, or until they test done with a cake tester or straw and are brown on top. Yields: 12 large muffins.

Pumpkin Chocolate Chip Muffins

4 eggs	3-1/2 cups flour
2 cups white sugar	1 Tablespoon cinnamon
1-1/2 cups oil	2 teaspoon baking soda
16 oz can pumpkin	2 teaspoon baking powder
Cloves (optional)	1 teaspoon salt
2 cups chocolate chips	Ginger (optional)

In large mixing bowl beat eggs, sugar, pumpkin and oil until smooth. Mix dry ingredients together and mix into pumpkin mixture. Fold in chocolate chips. Fill greased or paper-lined muffin cups 3/4 full. Bake at 400° F for 16-20 minutes. Yields: about 24 muffins.

Basic Pumpkin Muffins

1/3 cup vegetable oil
1 egg, beaten
1/4 cup milk
2/3 cup pureed cooked pumpkin
(canned or fresh)
1 cup sugar

1 cup all-purpose flour
3/4 teaspoon baking soda
1/2 teaspoon salt
1/4 teaspoon cinnamon
1/4 teaspoon nutmeg
1/4 teaspoon ginger

Preheat oven to 350°. In a bowl, combine butter, beaten egg, milk, and pumpkin. Beat well. Stir together all of the remaining dry ingredients and stir to creamy consistency. Do not beat. Fill greased muffin pans 2/3 foil and bake 25 to 30 minutes for regular muffins (or 15 to 20 for mini-muffins) until lightly browned. Remove from pan and serve warm.

Pumpkin Honey Muffins

1/2 cup margarine
1/2 cup sugar
1/4 cup honey
2 eggs
1-1/2 cups pumpkin puree

1 teaspoon lemon rind
2-1/2 cups self-raising flour
1/2 cup chopped pecans
1/2 cup yogurt

TOPPING
1 Tablespoon
2 Tablespoons sugar

1 teaspoon cinnamon

Preheat oven to 350° F; prepare pans. Blend margarine, sugar and honey. Beat in the eggs, yogurt, pumpkin and rind. Fold in flour until just combined. Spoon into pans and place a little of the topping on each muffin, press down very slightly. Bake for 20-25 minutes taking care not to scorch the topping. Makes: 12.

Pumpkin & Poppy Seed Muffins

1/2 cup cooked, pumpkin
1/2 cup milk
4-1/2 oz butter
3/4 cup sugar

1 egg
1/3 cup poppy seeds
2 cups self-raising flour

Preheat oven to 375° F; prepare pans. Cream butter and 1/2 cup, sugar, add egg and beat until light and creamy. Add milk then fold in pumpkin, pumpkin seeds, and then flour. Spoon into pans and sprinkle each muffin with the remaining sugar. Bake for 25 minutes.

Makes: 12.

Blueberry Pumpkin Muffins

1-2/3 cups flour
1 teaspoon baking soda
1/2 teaspoon baking powder
1/2 teaspoon salt
1 teaspoon cinnamon
1/2 teaspoon allspice
1 cup canned pumpkin

1/4 cup evaporated milk
1/3 cup butter
1 cup packed light brown sugar
1 egg
1 cup blueberries
1 Tablespoon flour

For Streusel Topping: Combine 2 Tablespoons each of flour and sugar, and 1/4 teaspoon cinnamon. Cut in 1 tablespoon, butter until mixture is crumbly.

Preheat oven to 350° F; prepare pans. Combine first 6 ingredients. Combine pumpkin and evaporated milk until blended. Cream shortening and sugar in large mixing bowl, add egg, beat until mixture is fluffy; mix in pumpkin mixture. Add flour mixture to wet mix until just combined. Coat the blueberries with the tablespoon of flour and gently mix into mixture. Spoon into pans; sprinkle with streusel topping. Bake for about 40 minutes or until toothpick inserted in center comes out clean.

Makes: 12-18 muffins.

Pumpkin Empanadas

FILLING
1-3/4 cups pumpkin puree
3/4 cup granulated sugar
1 teaspoon ground allspice

TOPPING
1/2 teaspoon ground cinnamon
1/4 cup sugar

CRUST
4 cups all-purpose flour
1/2 cup sugar
4 teaspoons baking powder
1 cup plus 2 tablespoons milk
1 teaspoon salt
1-1/3 cups shortening
1 egg white, beaten

Filling:
Combine pumpkin, sugar, and allspice; stir well, and set aside.

Crust:
Combine dry ingredients. With a fork, or pastry knife, cut in shortening until mixture resembles coarse meal. Sprinkle 1 cup of the milk evenly; stir until all dry ingredients are moistened. Shape into a ball; chill. Roll out to 1/8 inch thickness; cut into 4 inch circles.

Place one tablespoon of pumpkin mixture in the center of each circle. Moisten edges from the extra 2 tablespoons milk; fold in half, and press edges together with a fork. Brush empanadas with egg white; place on un-greased baking sheets, and bake at 450 degrees F. for 8 to 10 minutes or until golden. Combine 1/4 cup, sugar and cinnamon; sprinkle over empanadas while still warm.

Hot-Pepper Pumpkin Scones

1 stick, unsalted butter
1/2 small onion, chopped
1 jalapeno pepper
2 cups flour
2 teaspoon baking powder
1/2 teaspoon baking soda
1/2 teaspoon cinnamon
1/4 teaspoon ground ginger

1/8 teaspoon ground allspice
1/4 teaspoon salt
1/4 cup sugar
3/4 cup pumpkin puree
6 Tablespoons buttermilk
1 egg
1/4 cup honey
1 Tablespoon hot sauce

Preheat oven to 375° F. In a small skillet, melt the butter over medium heat, add onion, chopped finely and a jalapeno, that has been stemmed, seeded, and finely diced and stir until onion is soft. Set aside to cool.

In a large bowl, mix the flour, baking powder, soda, cinnamon, ginger, allspice, salt, and sugar. Mix in the melted butter until mixture resembles grams of rice. Make a well in the center and add buttermilk, pumpkin puree and egg to the well. Mix together with a fork, gradually working in the mixture until a soft dough forms. Drop the batter 1/3 cupful at a time 2 inches apart on a lightly greased cookie sheet. Bake in a preheated oven for 20 minutes, until puffed and firm on surface, but fluffy in the center.

Transfer to a cooling rack, cover loosely with a dish towel and cool for at least 5 minutes. Mix honey with the jalapeno sauce and brush tops of the scones with this mixture before serving.

Colonists sliced off pumpkin tops; removed seeds and filled the insides with milk, spices and honey. This was baked in hot ashes and is the origin of pumpkin pie.

Pumpkin Biscuits

1/2 cup hot milk	1 teaspoon salt
2 Tablespoons butter	3-1/4 cups all purpose flour
3 Tablespoons sugar	1 Tablespoon active dry yeast
1/2 cup pureed pumpkin	1/4 cup warm water

Combine hot milk, butter, sugar, pumpkin, salt and 1/4 cup flour in a large bowl. Stir yeast into 1/4 cup warm water and let stand for 5 minutes or until bubbly. Add yeast to the first mixture and beat vigorously. Cover and leave in a warm place to rise for 30 minutes or until light.

Stir in 2 to 3 cups flour until dough leaves sides of bowl. Turn out onto a floured surface and knead in flour until dough is smooth and elastic, about 8 minutes. Place dough in a greased bowl and turn it once to grease the top. Cover and place in a warm draft-free place until doubled in size, about 45 minutes.

Punch dough down, and turn out onto a lightly floured board. Roll dough with a rolling pin to 1/4 inch thickness. Cut into 2 inch rounds. Place rounds about 1 inch apart on greased baking sheets. Cover and let rise for 20 minutes or until almost double in size. Bake on the middle rack in a preheated 400° F. oven for 10 to 12 minutes or until golden brown.

Overnight Herbed Pumpkin Dinner Rolls

2 teaspoons coarse salt
2 eggs, room temperature
1 cup pumpkin puree
1/2 cup butter, room temperature
1/2 cup sugar
2 Tablespoons melted butter
2 (1/4-ounce) envelopes active dry yeast
1/4 cup warm water (110 to 115 degrees)

1 Tablespoon minced fresh thyme
(or 1 teaspoon dried)
1/4 teaspoon cayenne pepper
3 cups flour, plus 1 cup more
Olive oil, for greasing bowl

Sprinkle the yeast over the water in a large mixing bowl and stir to dissolve. With a wooden spoon, beat in eggs, pumpkin, soft butter, sugar, salt, thyme and cayenne. Add 3 cups of flour and beat until smooth, gradually adding more flour as needed to make a soft sticky but still manageable dough. Oil a larger bowl and scrape dough into it, turning to oil all sides. Cover with a dishtowel and let rise in a warm, draft-free area until doubled, about 1-1/2 hours. Punch the dough down, cover tightly with plastic wrap and refrigerate overnight.

In two 8 inch cake pans, greased with melted butter. Punch the dough down again and shape into round dinner rolls, arranging them in pans with about half an inch between each (if the dough is too sticky to handle easily, lightly butter or oil your hands). Cover rolls with a towel and let rise in a warm spot until doubled, 30 minutes.

Heat the oven to 375° F. Bake until browned, 20 to 25 minutes. Serve hot or warm.

Quick & Easy Pumpkin Pancakes

2 cups flour
2 Tablespoons sugar
4 teaspoon baking powder
1 teaspoon salt
1 teaspoon cinnamon

1-1/2 cups milk
1 cup pumpkin puree
4 eggs, separated
1/4 cup melted butter

Sift dry ingredients together. Combine milk, egg yolks, butter and pumpkin puree. Stir into dry ingredients until just blended. Beat egg whites until stiff and fold into batter. Pour on to hot, oiled griddle, about 1/3 cup at a time. Cook until tops bubble and turn and cook other side.

Pumpkin Oat Pancakes

1 cup all-purpose flour
1 cup quick-cooking oats
2 Tablespoons wheat germ
2 teaspoons sugar
2 teaspoons baking powder
1/2 teaspoon salt

Pinch ground cinnamon
1 cup milk
1 egg, lightly beaten
3/4 cup canned pumpkin
2 Tablespoons vegetable oil

In a mixing bowl, combine the flour, oats, wheat germ, sugar, baking powder, salt and cinnamon. Combine milk, egg, pumpkin and oil; stir into dry ingredients just until moistened. Pour batter by 1/4 cupfuls onto a hot greased griddle; turn when bubbles form on top of pancakes. Cook until second side is golden brown. YIELD: 10-12 pancakes

Pumpkin Pancakes

1 cup whole wheat flour
1 Tablespoon baking powder
1/2 teaspoon salt
1/4 teaspoon cinnamon

1 egg
1 cup milk
1/2 cup pumpkin puree
1 Tablespoon Canola oil

In large bowl, add dry ingredients together and set aside. In a separate bowl beat together egg, milk, pumpkin, and oil. Add to dry ingredients, stir and combine. Do not over mix. Drop by spoonful onto preheated nonstick skillet. Cook on medium to medium-high heat until bubbles appear on surface. Flip and cook other side. Makes: 10, 5 inch pancakes.

Whole Grain Pumpkin Bread

1 cup oil or butter
1-1/2 cup light brown sugar
1/2 cup molasses
2 eggs, well beaten
16 oz can pumpkin
2 cups flour
1/2 cup whole wheat flour
1/3 cup wheat bran

1/3 cup oat bran
1/3 cup wheat germ
2 teaspoons baking soda
2 teaspoons cinnamon
1 teaspoon cloves
1 teaspoon nutmeg
1/2 teaspoon salt
1/4 cup pecans, chopped

This recipe uses a lot of whole grains, but it will turn out great if you have to use all-purpose flour in place of any or all of the whole grains. Any of the whole grains are can be exchanged with any of the other whole grains in the recipe. Preheat oven to 375° F. Grease 2 loaf pans. Beat oil, brown sugar, and molasses until well blended. Blend in egg and pumpkin. Stir flours, bran, wheat germ, soda, cinnamon, cloves, nutmeg, and salt into mixture just until moistened. Fold in nuts. Fill pans and bake about 1 hour, until pick comes out clean. Cool on rack. Better if served the day after cooking. Freezes well.

Pumpkin Raisin Bread

1-2/3 cups flour
1 teaspoon baking soda
1/4 teaspoon baking powder
3/4 teaspoon salt
1/2 teaspoon ground cloves
1-1/2 teaspoon ground cinnamon
1 cup raisins

1/2 teaspoon ground nutmeg
1/2 teaspoon ground allspice
3/4 cup sugar
1/2 cup margarine
2 eggs
1 cup canned pumpkin

Sift flour, soda, powder, salt and spices. In another bowl beat the sugar and oil until smooth. Beat in eggs one at a time. Stir in pumpkin and flour mixture. Add raisins. Turn into loaf pan. Bake at 350° for 60 minutes. Makes: one loaf.

Hazelnut Spice Pumpkin Bread

4 cups pumpkin
2 Tablespoons water
4 cups brown sugar
1 cup vegetable oil
5 cups flour
1-2 oz. rum
1 teaspoon lemon zest
1 teaspoon orange zest
1/2 cup chopped dried apricots

4 teaspoons cinnamon
1 teaspoon cloves
1/14 teaspoon nutmeg
1/4 teaspoon allspice
4 teaspoons soda
1 teaspoon salt
1 cup golden raisins
1 cup chopped hazelnuts

Stir pumpkin, water, oil, sugar, and spices together, mixing well. Sift flour, salt, and soda and stir into liquid mixture. Add rum, fruits and nuts. Pour into greased 1-quart loaf pans. Bake at 350° for 1 hour or until the toothpick comes out clean. Cool before slicing.

Easy Pumpkin Bread

3 cups sugar
1 cup oil
4 eggs, slightly beaten
1 can pumpkin
3-1/2 cups all-purpose flour
2 teaspoons baking soda
1 teaspoon baking powder

2 teaspoons salt
1 teaspoon nutmeg
1 teaspoon allspice
1 teaspoon cinnamon
1/2 teaspoon ground cloves
2/3 cup water

Preheat oven to 350° F. In a large bowl, mix sugar and oil. Add pumpkin and eggs. Blend well. Add flour, spices, and water. Mix completely. Pour into two, well-greased loaf pans. Bake for 1-1/2 hours or until toothpick inserted in center comes out clean.

Seminole Pumpkin Bread

2 cups pumpkin puree
4 cups all-purpose flour
4 teaspoons baking powder
1 teaspoon baking soda

1 cup water
1/2 cup white sugar
Oil for frying
White sugar

Sift flour, baking powder and baking soda together. Gradually add pumpkin, sugar and water to form a soft dough. When it just holds together, knead several minutes. Divide dough into 4-6 equal parts. Knead each portion again several minutes or until it becomes a soft, smooth ball. Roll out each portion 1/4 inch thick, or pinch off small pieces of dough and form into individual cakes 2 to 3 inches across. Fry in very hot oil about 1 inch deep, browning on both sides. Bread will puff up and become crispy and chewy. Sprinkle with granulated sugar.

Walnut/Butter Pumpkin Bread

2 cups all-purpose flour	1 teaspoon ground cinnamon
1 cup packed brown sugar	1/4 teaspoon ground nutmeg
1 Tablespoon baking powder	1/8 teaspoon ground ginger
1/4 teaspoon baking soda	1/2 cup chopped walnuts
1/2 cup milk	1 cup raisins
1 cup pumpkin puree	1/4 teaspoon salt
2 eggs	1/2 cup sweet butter

In a large mixer bowl combine 1 cup of flour, brown sugar, baking powder, cinnamon, salt, baking soda, nutmeg, and ginger. Add pumpkin, milk, eggs, and shortening. Beat with an electric mixer on low speed till blended, then on high speed for 2 minutes. Add remaining flour, beat well. Stir in nuts and raisins. Pour batter into a greased 9 x 5 x 3 inch loaf pan. Bake in a 350° F oven for 60 to 65 minutes or until a toothpick inserted near the center comes out clean. Cool for 10 minutes on a wire rack. Remove from the pan; cool thoroughly.

Cranberry Pumpkin Bread

2-1/4 cups all-purpose flour	2 eggs
1 Tablespoon Pumpkin Pie Spice	1/2 cup vegetable oil
1 Tablespoon baking soda	1 cup solid pack pumpkin
1/2 teaspoon salt	1 cup cranberries, chopped
2 cups sugar	

Preheat oven to 350° F. In a large bowl, combine flour, pumpkin pie spice, baking soda and salt, in a small mixer bowl, beat eggs; beat in sugar, oil and pumpkin. Pour pumpkin mix into the dry ingredients; stir just until moistened. Stir in cranberries. Spoon batter into two greased and floured 8 x 4 inch loaf pans. Bake for 60 minutes or until wooden pick comes out clean. Cool 5 to 10 minutes; remove from pans.

Pumpkin Pinion Nut Sweetbread

1-1/2 cups unbleached four
1 cup pureed pumpkin
3/4 cup brown sugar
1/2 cup melted butter (1 stick)
2 eggs, beaten foamy

1 teaspoon baking powder
1 teaspoon cinnamon
1 teaspoon grated nutmeg
1/2 teaspoon salt
3/4 cup pine nuts

Preheat oven to 350 F. In a mixing bowl, combine flour, salt, baking powder, sugar and spices. Stir in pumpkin, eggs and butter. Stir pine nuts into thick batter. Scrape into a greased 6 x 9 inch loaf pan. Bake for 1 hour or until a knife inserted in bread comes out clean.

Pumpkin Pecan Bread

1 cup butter, softened
1 cup granulated sugar
1 cup brown sugar, packed
4 eggs
1 cup canned pumpkin
1 cup pecans, chopped

2-3/4 cup all-purpose flour
1 Tablespoon pumpkin pie spice
2 teaspoons baking powder
1 teaspoon baking soda
1/2 teaspoon salt

Cream butter and sugars in large mixer bowl until light. Add eggs, one at a time, beating well after each addition. Beat in pumpkin. Combine flour, pumpkin pie spice, baking powder, baking soda, salt, and pecans in a small bowl. Add to pumpkin mixture; mix until blended. Spoon into 2 greased and floured 8-1/2 by 4-1/2 inch loaf pans. Bake in preheated oven at 350° F for 1 hour and 10 minutes or until toothpick comes out clean from center. Cool 10 minutes and remove from pans and finish cooling on wire rack.

Banana Pumpkin Bread

1/2 cup applesauce
2 egg whites, whipped
3 Tablespoons orange juice
1 cup bananas, mashed
1/2 cup pumpkin
2-1/2 cups all-purpose flour
1/2 cup sugar

1/2 cup brown sugar, packed
1 Tablespoon cinnamon
1/8 Tablespoon cloves
1 Tablespoon baking powder
1/2 Tablespoon baking soda
1/2 cup raisins

Preheat oven to 350°F. Prepare a pan with cooking spray and flour. In mixing bowl, combine applesauce, egg whites, orange juice, bananas, and pumpkin. In another mixing bowl, combine flour, sugars, cinnamon, cloves, baking powder, baking soda, and raisins. Mix wet ingredients with dry ingredients just until moistened. Pour into prepared pan. Bake for 1-1/4 hours depending on pan size.

Old Fashioned Pumpkin Bread

1 cup white sugar
1 cup dark brown sugar
1-1/4 teaspoon salt
3 teaspoons baking Soda
1 cup oil
4 eggs
2/3 cup water
3-1/2 cups sifted flour

2 cups pumpkin
1 teaspoon nutmeg
1/2 teaspoon ground cloves
1 teaspoon cinnamon
2 Tablespoons molasses
1 cup raisins
1 cup chopped nuts

Combine all ingredients and mix vigorously. Divide batter into 3, 8-1/2 x 4-1/2 inch greased and floured loaf pans. In a preheated oven, bake at 350° F for about 1 to 1-1/2 hours until a toothpick inserted, comes out clean. Cool in pans on wire rack. Yields: 3 loaves.

Native Americans flattened strips of pumpkins; dried them and made mats.

Pumpkin Date Nut Bread

1 cup flour	1 cup cooked pumpkin
1 cup oat flour	1/3 cup cream
1/2 teaspoon baking powder	1/3 cup brandy
1 teaspoon baking soda	1/2 teaspoon ginger powder
1 teaspoon allspice	1/2 teaspoon ground cloves
1/2 teaspoon salt	1/2 teaspoon vanilla
1-1/3 cup sugar	1/2 cup dates, chopped
1/2 cup softened butter	2 teaspoons cinnamon
2 eggs	1/2 cup walnuts, finely ground
1/4 cup pecans, finely ground	

Combine flour and oat flour, leavenings, and spices in one bowl. Beat sugar, eggs and butter until light and creamy in a large mixing bowl. Add pumpkin and thoroughly blend. Add all of the dry ingredients, and cream and brandy alternately, to egg mixture. Stir in vanilla and pour the batter into a greased loaf pan and bake at 350° F for 1 hour or until bread is done.

Swirled Surprise Pumpkin Bread

8 oz. cream cheese	1 teaspoon ground cinnamon
1/4 cup white sugar	1/2 teaspoon salt
2 eggs, beaten, but not together	1/4 teaspoon nutmeg
1-3/4 cups all-purpose flour	1 cup pumpkin puree
1-1/2 cups white sugar	1/2 cup butter, melted
1 teaspoon baking soda	1/3 cup water

Blend cream cheese, 1/4 cup sugar, and 1 beaten egg. Set aside. Combine flour, sugar, baking soda, salt, and spices. Set aside. Combine pumpkin, butter or margarine, the second beaten egg and water. Add flour mixture to pumpkin mixture, mixing just until moistened. Reserve 2 cups of the pumpkin batter. Pour the remaining batter into a greased and floured 9 x 5 inch loaf pan. Pour cream cheese mixture over pumpkin batter, and top with reserved pumpkin batter. Cut through batter several times with a knife for a swirl effect. Bake at 350° F for 70 minutes, or until tester comes out clean. Cool in the pan for 10 minutes; remove from pan to cool completely.

Special Coconut Pumpkin Bread

1-1/4 cups vegetable oil
2 cups pumpkin puree
1 cup brown sugar
1 cup white sugar
2 packages instant
coconut pudding mix

1 teaspoon ground cinnamon
1 teaspoon salt
5 eggs
2 cups all-purpose flour
1 teaspoon baking soda
1 cup chopped nuts

In a large bowl, mix together oil, pumpkin, sugars, pudding mixes, cinnamon, and salt. Slightly beat the eggs, and mix into the batter. Mix in flour and baking soda until just combined. Stir in nuts and spread batter into two greased and floured 9x5 inch loaf pans. Bake at 325° F for 1 hour, or until a knife inserted in the center comes out clean.

Pumpkin Bread

3-1/3 cups flour
4 teaspoons pumpkin pie spice
2 teaspoons baking soda
1 teaspoon baking powder
1-1/2 teaspoon salt
2-2/3 cups sugar

4 large eggs
2 cups pumpkin, canned
2/3 cup water
2/3 cup dates, chopped
2/3 cup walnuts, chopped
2/3 cup cooking oil

Preheat oven to 325° F. Stir flour, pumpkin pie spice, baking soda, baking powder, and salt together in a bowl; set aside. Using an electric mixer set on high, beat sugar and oil together until light and fluffy. Add eggs, one at a time beating well after each addition. Beat in pumpkin. Add dry ingredients and water alternately to the sugar mixture, beating well with mixer on low speed.

Stir in dates and pour the batter into, 2 greased 9 x 5 x 3 inch loaf pans. Bake 55 minutes, or until a toothpick inserted in the center comes out clean. Cool 10 minutes before removing from pans, then continue cooling on the racks.

Pumpkin Swirl Bread

FILLING

1/4 cup sugar	4 ounces cream cheese
1 cup sour cream	1 egg

BREAD

2-2/3 cups sugar	1 teaspoon cinnamon
1 cup vegetable oil	1/2 teaspoon ground ginger
1/3 cup water	1/2 teaspoon ground nutmeg
1 16 oz can pumpkin	1/2 teaspoon salt
4 eggs	2 teaspoons baking soda
3-1/2 cups all-purpose flour	

Heat oven to 350° F. In a small mixer bowl combine all filling ingredients. Beat at medium speed, scraping bowl often, until well mixed; set aside. In a large mixer bowl combine sugar, oil, water, pumpkin and eggs and beat at low speed, scraping sides of bowl often, until mixture is smooth. Continue beating at medium speed, gradually adding all remaining ingredients until well mixed. Place 1/4, (about 2 cups) pumpkin batter into bottom of each of 2 greased and floured 9 x 5 inch loaf pans. Carefully spread 1/2 of the filling mixture over batter in each pan; top each with half of the remaining pumpkin batter. Pull knife through batter and filling to create swirl effect. Bake for 65 to 70 minutes or until toothpick inserted in center comes out clean. Cool 10 minutes; remove from pans. Cool completely.

Pumpkin Almond Bread

1/2 cup oil	1-1/2 cup flour
2/3 cup brown sugar	1/2 teaspoon baking powder
1/3 cup sugar	1 teaspoon baking soda
1 cup pumpkin puree	1/2 teaspoon salt
1 egg	1/2 teaspoon ginger
1 Tablespoon orange rind grated	1/2 cup toasted almond slivers

Beat together the first 6 ingredients. Combine and sift the dry ingredients and add to mixture. Stir in the almonds last. Grease and floured 1 loaf pan and bake at 350° F. for 1 hr.

Golden Pumpkin Bread

16 oz can pumpkin
1-1/2 cups sugar
1 cup packed brown sugar
4 eggs
1/2 cup vegetable oil
3-1/2 cups flour
1 cup enriched corn meal
2 teaspoons baking soda

2 teaspoons salt
2 teaspoons pumpkin pie spice
1 teaspoon baking powder
1 cup sour cream
1/2 cup water
3/4 cup raisins
1/2 cup chopped pecans

Preheated oven to 350° F. Beat together pumpkin, sugars, eggs and oil. Combine dry ingredients and add to pumpkin mixture; alternating with sour cream and water, mixing well after each addition. Stir in raisins and pecans. Pour into two well-greased 9 x 5 inch loaf pans. Bake about 1 hour and 10 minutes. Cool 10 minutes and remove from pans. If using small loaf pans bake 40 to 45 minutes

Orange Pumpkin Loaf

1/3 cup butter
1-1/3 cups white sugar
2 eggs
1 cup canned pumpkin
1/3 cup water
1 medium size orange
2 cups all-purpose flour

1 teaspoon baking soda
1/2 teaspoon baking powder
3/4 teaspoon salt
1/2 teaspoon ground cinnamon
1/2 teaspoon ground cloves
1/2 cup chopped nuts
1/2 cup raisins

Preheat oven to 350° F. Cream butter and sugar together, add eggs, beating lightly. Stir in pumpkin and water. Cut and remove seeds from orange. Put in blender or grinder and grind complete orange including peel and stir into batter. In a separate bowl, combine flour, soda, baking powder, salt, cinnamon, cloves, nuts, and raisins. Mix well. Stir dry ingredients into batter. Spoon into greased 9 x 5 x 3 inch loaf pan. Bake 1 hour, or until toothpick inserted into center comes out clean. Let cool 10 minutes before removing from pan.

Spicy Low Fat Pumpkin Bread

1/2 teaspoon salt
1 teaspoon cinnamon
1/2 teaspoon nutmeg
1/2 teaspoon ginger
1/4 teaspoon allspice
1/4 powdered cloves
1/2 cup currants

1/2 cup applesauce
1 cup cooked, pureed pumpkin
2 egg whites
1/3 cup water
1-3/4 cups flour
1 teaspoon baking soda
1 cup sugar

Beat together first four ingredients. Add baking soda, sugar and salt. Mix. Stir in flour and mix until just combined. Add all spices and currants. Stir in. Spray 3 baby loaf pans with cooking spray and fill each about 2/3 full. Bake at 350° F degrees for 45 minutes

Wheat & Dairy Free Pumpkin Bread

1-1/2 cups bean flour
1-1/2 cups rice flour
1-1/2 teaspoons salt
1 teaspoon ground cinnamon
1 teaspoon nutmeg
2 teaspoons baking soda

3 teaspoons xanthan gum
2 cups pureed pumpkin
1 cup honey
1 cup corn oil
1/2 cup water
4 eggs

Grease and flour 2 loaf pans. Stir together flour, sugar, baking soda, salt and spices. Stir together pumpkin, corn oil and water, then, add eggs one at a time. Make a well in center of flour mixture; add pumpkin mixture and stir. Pour into prepared pans and bake for 1 hour at 325°F.

Pumpkin Pumpernickel Bread

1-1/2 cups cold water	1 package yeast
3/4 cup corn meal	1/4 cup lukewarm water
1-1/2 cups boiling water	2 cups mashed pumpkin
1-1/2 Tablespoons salt	6 cups rye flour
2 Tablespoons sugar	2 cups whole wheat flour
1 Tablespoon caraway seeds	2 Tablespoons shortening

Stir cold water into cornmeal. Add to boiling water and cook stirring constantly until thick. Add salt, sugar, caraway seeds. Let stand till lukewarm. Meanwhile; soften yeast in lukewarm water. After 15 minutes, stir pumpkin and yeast into cornmeal dough. Add rye flour and enough whole wheat to make a stiff dough. You have to stir with your hands.

Turn dough out onto floured board and knead for 10 to 15 minutes until it becomes elastic and doesn't stick to the board. Place dough in large greased bowl, grease its surface and set in warm place (80 to 85°) to rise until doubled (takes longer than white or whole-wheat breads; set in metal bowl in dishpan or bigger bowl of hot water to help it along).

Punch down and form into 3 rounded ball shaped loaves. Grease tops and let rise again until doubled in bulk. Bake in preheated 375° oven about 1 hour.

Pumpkin Spice Ring

1 box angel food cake mix	1 cup pumpkin puree
1/2 teaspoon pumpkin pie spice	

Combine pumpkin and pumpkin pie spice, and mix well. Set aside. Mix cake as directed on package. Fold in pumpkin mixture. Pour into an un-greased tube pan. Bake at 350° F. until lightly browned, using the box directions as a guide to cooking time.

Pumpkin Mincemeat Bread

3-1/2 cups sifted flour
2 Tablespoons pumpkin pie spice
1-1/2 teaspoon salt
4 eggs, slightly beaten
2/3 cup water
1 cup salad oil

1-1/2 cups white sugar
2 teaspoons baking soda
1-1/2 cups packed brown sugar
2 cups pumpkin puree
9 oz. box dry mincemeat
1 cup chopped walnuts

Into a large bowl, sift flour, white sugar, pumpkin pie spice, baking soda and salt. Mix in brown sugar. Make a well in the center; add eggs, water, oil and pumpkin. Beat at low speed until ingredients are blended, then, beat at medium-high speed about three minutes. Divide dough into four 1-pound coffee cans and bake at 350° F 50 to 60 minutes, or use 3, 8-1/2 x 4-1/2 x 2-1/2 inch loaf pans; baking 55 to 65 minutes. For 2 , 9 -1/2 x 5-1/2 x 2-3/4 inch loaf pans, bake 60 to 70 minutes.

Note:
When I tried this recipe and used mincemeat from a jar. It turned out great.

Pumpkin Bread with Orange Sauce

3-1/2 cups flour
2 teaspoons baking soda
1 teaspoon salt
1 teaspoon cinnamon
1 teaspoon nutmeg
1 teaspoon cloves
1 teaspoon allspice

3 cups sugar
1 cup vegetable oil
4 eggs, beat lightly
2 cups pumpkin
2/3 cup water
1-1/2 cup chopped pecans

Preheat oven to 350° F. In large bowl, combine flour, baking soda, salt, spices, and sugar. Add oil, eggs, pumpkin, and water, beating until well blended. Stir in pecans. Put into two lightly greased 9 x 5 x 5 inch loaf pans. Bake 1 hour or until toothpick comes out clean. Remove from pans and cool on wire racks. (Serve with orange sauce.)

ORANGE SAUCE:

Juice from one orange
1 Tablespoon lemon juice
1 cup water
1/2 cup granulated sugar

3 Tablespoons cornstarch
Grated rind from one orange
1 egg, beat lightly
1 teaspoon butter

In medium microwave proof bowl, combine orange and lemon juice with water, then, add sugar and cornstarch, stirring until dissolved. Stir in grated orange rind, egg and butter. Cook, in microwave on high for about 5 minutes, or until mixture boils and thickens. Allow sauce to cool; store in airtight container in refrigerator. Serve warm or cold.

Note:
This recipe not only tastes good, but looks great also and makes and excellent gift.

Native Americans used pumpkin seeds for food and medicine.

Pumpkin Doughnuts

3-1/2 cups all purpose flour
1 Tablespoon baking powder
1 teaspoon baking soda
1 teaspoon salt
1/2 teaspoon ground ginger
3/4 cup sugar

2 eggs
2/3 cup pumpkin puree
2/3 cup buttermilk
1/2 teaspoon cinnamon
1/4 cup butter, softened
Vegetable oil (for deep flying)

GLAZE
1/2 cup maple sugar

1/2 cup sugar

Sift flour with baking powder, soda, salt, cinnamon and ginger into medium bowl. Using an electric mixer, cream butter in large bowl until fluffy. Gradually add 3/4 cup sugar and beat until fluffy. Add eggs, one at a time, beating well after each addition. Beat in 1/4 cup dry ingredients. Add pumpkin and buttermilk and mix thoroughly. Add remaining dry ingredients and stir until just blended (dough will be sticky). Cover and refrigerate at least 3 hours.

Combine maple sugar and 1/2 cup sugar in paper bad. Set aside. Roll dough out on lightly floured surface to thickness of 1/4 to 1/3 inch. Using lightly floured 3 1/2 inch doughnut cutter (or 3-inch-round cookie cutter and 1-inch-round cookie cutter for center hole), cut out doughnuts and doughnut holes. Transfer to floured board. Let stand 10 minutes.

Heat, 4 inches of oil in deep fryer or heavy saucepan to 365 ° F. Cook doughnuts and doughnut holes until golden brown, turning once. Transfer to paper towels using slotted spoon and drain 3 minutes. Immediately transfer to paper bag containing sugar mixture. Shake to coat. Arrange on racks to cool.

Pumpkin Eaters Doughnuts

2 Tablespoons shortening
3/4 cup sugar
2 eggs
1 cup solid pack pumpkin
1 cup shredded bran cereal

2~3/4 cups flour
2 teaspoons baking powder
1 teaspoon pumpkin pie spice
1/2 teaspoon salt
Oil

In a large bowl, cream shortening and sugar until light and fluffy. Add eggs, one at a time mixing well after each. Add pumpkin and cereal, mixing well. Let stand 2 minutes. Sift flour, baking powder, spice and salt together then stir into pumpkin mixture. Cover, chill for 1 hour or until dough is stiff enough to handle. On lightly floured surface, roll out dough to 1/2 in. thickness and cut with 2-1/2 in doughnut cutter. Deep fry in a large pan, with 2 inches of oil at: 375° F. Fry a few at a time about 1 minute per side or until thoroughly cooked and golden brown. Drain on paper towel on wire rack. Repeat with the trimmings to use all of the dough. Dip cooled doughnuts in cinnamon sugar or powdered sugar if desired.

Pumpkin Crunch Cake

1 16 oz. can pumpkin
1 12 oz. can evaporated milk
3 eggs, slightly beaten
1-1/2 cups sugar
4 teaspoons Pumpkin Pie Spice

1/2 teaspoon salt
1 box yellow cake mix
1 cup chopped pecans
1 cup melted butter

Combine pumpkin, evaporated milk, eggs, sugar, Pumpkin Pie Spice, and salt. Mix with a spoon, not an electric mixer. Pour into 13 x 9 inch pan, greased only on the bottom. Spread cake mix (dry mix only) evenly over pumpkin. Sprinkle pecans over cake mix and pour melted butter over top. Bake at 350° F. for 55 to 60 minutes.

Pumpkin Pound Cake

2 cups packed light brown sugar	1 teaspoon nutmeg
2 cups margarine or butter	1 teaspoon salt
4 cups all-purpose flour	6 large eggs
2 teaspoons baking soda	1 can pumpkin (16-oz.)
2 teaspoons cinnamon	

Preheat oven to 325° F. Grease two 9 x 5 inch loaf pans. In a large bowl, beat brown sugar and butter until blended, with mixer at low speed. Increase speed to high; beat until light and fluffy. Reduce speed to low; add flour, baking soda, cinnamon, ginger, nutmeg, salt, eggs and pumpkin; beat until well mixed, scraping bowl frequently with rubber spatula. Increase speed to high; beat 2 minutes, occasionally scraping bowl. Spoon batter into pans! Bake loaves 70 to 75 minutes, until toothpick inserted in the center comes out clean. Cool loaves in pans on wire racks 10 minutes; remove from pans and finish cooling.

ORANGE SAUCE:

2 teaspoons ginger	2/3 cup confectioners' sugar
1 Tablespoon orange juice	

In a small bowl, mix confectioners' sugar with orange juice; drizzle over cooled loaves.

GARNISH - CANDIED ORANGE PEEL:
Candied orange peel

With vegetable peeler, peel 1 inch wide long strips of peel from 2 large oranges. Trim off as much white membrane from peel as possible. In a one quart. saucepan over high heat, heat orange peel strips, 3/4 cup water, and 1/3 cup sugar to boiling. Reduce heat to low; simmer 15 minutes, stirring occasionally until orange peel is limp and translucent. Drain orange peel and place on cookie sheet; sprinkle randomly with 1 teaspoon sugar. Let dry. Sprinkle over loves as a garnish, or on top of cut pieces.

Pumpkin Cake Roll

3 eggs, beaten
1 cup sugar
1 teaspoon lemon juice
2/3 cup pumpkin
3/4 cup flour

1 teaspoon baking powder
2 teaspoons cinnamon
1/2 teaspoon nutmeg
1 teaspoon ginger

Beat eggs add sugar, lemon juice, and pumpkin. Mix well. Blend dry ingredients together and add to mixture. Beat well. Put waxed paper on cookie sheet, grease with cooking spray. Pour batter on top and bake 375 °° F. for 15 minutes. While still warm, put a towel on top of cake and roll up. When cool, unroll enough to frost with filler frosting.

FILLER FROSTING:
1 cup powdered sugar
8 oz. softened cream cheese

4 Tablespoons butter
1 teaspoon vanilla

Mix above ingredients well and spread over the unrolled cake. Roll up, again, and refrigerate until cheese sets. (2 or 3 hours) Slice and serve!

Pumpkin Upside Down Cake

1 cup granulated sugar
3 eggs, beaten
3-1/2 cups canned pumpkin
2 teaspoons ground cinnamon
1/2 teaspoon ground ginger
1/4 teaspoon ground cloves

1/2 teaspoon salt
1-1/2 oz. can evaporated milk
1 yellow cake mix
1 cup chopped nuts
4 Tablespoons butter, melted
Whipped cream

Preheat oven to 350° F. Mix together sugar, eggs, pumpkin, cinnamon, ginger, cloves, salt and milk. Line a 9 x 13 inch pan with wax paper and pour in mixture. Sprinkle the dry cake mix on top, then, sprinkle nuts. Pour melted butter evenly over the cake mix and nuts. Bake for 50 to 60 minutes. Cool then flip over and remove from pan. Remove the wax paper. Top with whipped cream before serving.

Pumpkin Log

CAKE:

3 eggs
1 cup sugar
2/3 cup pumpkin

1 teaspoon baking soda
1 teaspoon cinnamon
3/4 cup flour

FILLING:

2 teaspoons margarine
8 ounces cream cheese

3/4 teaspoon vanilla
1 cup powdered sugar

Preheat oven to 350° F. Combine eggs, sugar, pumpkin, baking soda, cinnamon, and flour. Spread onto greased cookie sheet. Bake for 15 minutes. Turn onto a towel which has been sprinkled well with powdered sugar. Roll up jelly roll fashion. Let cool completely. Meanwhile combine filling ingredients. When cool unroll and spread on filling. Roll back and refrigerate.

Note:

If desired, sprinkle pecan pieces over spread filling before rolling.

Pumpkin Chocolate Chip Cake

1 can pumpkin puree
3 eggs
2 cups flour
2 cups sugar
1/2 teaspoon salt

1/2 teaspoon cinnamon
2 teaspoons baking powder
2 teaspoons baking soda
1 small bag chocolate chips

Preheat oven to 350° F. Grease and flower a tube pan. Combine all ingredients, except the chocolate chips, into a mixing bowl, mixing well. Blend in chocolate chips by hand, mixing. Pour mixture into the greased and floured tube pan Bake for one hour. Remove and allow cake to cool before serving.

Pumpkin Cookie Dip

1 8 oz package cream cheese
2 7 oz jars marshmallow cream
1 can solid pack pumpkin

1 teaspoon ground cinnamon
1 teaspoon grated orange peel

In a mixing bowl, beat the cream cheese and marshmallow cream until smooth. Stir in pumpkin, cinnamon and orange peel. Serve as a dip with cookies. Store in the refrigerator.

Pumpkin Vermont Spice Cake

1-1/2 cup sugar
3/4 cup butter, softened
3 eggs
1-1/2 cup pumpkin
1-1/2 teaspoon vanilla
1/2 cup evaporated milk
1/4 cup water
3 cups flour

3-1/2 teaspoons baking powder
1 teaspoon baking soda
1/2 teaspoon salt
1-1/2 teaspoon cinnamon
3/4 teaspoon nutmeg
1/4 teaspoon cloves
1/4 teaspoon ginger
15 walnut or pecan halves

Preheat oven to 325° F. Grease and flour two 9 inch round bake pans. Cream granulated sugar and 3/4 cup butter in mixer bowl. Add eggs; beat 2 minutes. Stir in pumpkin and vanilla, mixing well. Beat in evaporated milk and water. Combine flour, baking powder, baking soda, salt, cinnamon, nutmeg, cloves and ginger. Gradually beat all of the dry ingredients into pumpkin mixture. Spread evenly in prepared pans. Bake in preheated oven 35 to 40 minutes until wooden pick inserted in center comes out clean. Cool on wire racks 15 minutes. Remove from pans. Cool completely.

FROSTING:
11 oz. cream cheese, softened
1/3 cup butter, softened

3-1/2 cups powdered sugar
2 teaspoons maple flavoring

Beat cream cheese, butter and powdered sugar until fluffy. Add maple flavoring and mix well. Use long serrated knife to cut each cake in half horizontally. Frost between layers and on top of cake. To make a 2-layer cake, do not slice but frost between layers, over top, and on side of cake. Garnish with nuts.

89

Harvest Pumpkin Torte

4 eggs; separated
3/4 cup + 1 Tablespoon sugar
1/2 cup all-purpose flour
1/3 cup cocoa
Slivered almonds

1/2 teaspoon baking soda
1/4 teaspoon salt
1/3 cup water
1 teaspoon vanilla extract

Heat oven to 375° F. Line 15-1/2 x 10-1/2 inch jelly roll pan with foil; generously grease foil. In large mixer bowl, beat egg yolks on medium speed for 3 minutes; gradually add 1/2 cup sugar, beating 2 minutes. Stir together flour, cocoa, 1/4 cup sugar, baking soda and salt; add to egg yolk mixture alternately with water, while beating on low speed just until batter is smooth. Stir in vanilla; set aside. In small mixer bowl, beat egg whites until soft peaks form; gradually add remaining 1 tablespoon sugar, beating until stiff peaks form. Gradually fold beaten egg whites into chocolate mixture until well blended. Spread batter into prepared pan. Bake 14 to 16 minutes or until top springs back when touched lightly. Immediately loosen cake from edges of pan; invert onto clean, slightly dampened towel. Carefully peel off foil. Cool completely.

PUMPKIN FILLING:

3 Tablespoons shortening
1 teaspoon ground cinnamon
1/4 teaspoon ground nutmeg
1-3/4 cup powdered sugar

1 cup canned pumpkin
1/4 cup all-purpose flour
1/3 cup butter, softened

In small saucepan, combine pumpkin and flour; cook over medium heat, stirring constantly, until mixture boils (mixture will be very thick). Remove from heat; set aside. Cool completely. In small mixing bowl, beat butter and shortening until creamy; add spices. Gradually add powdered sugar, beating until light and fluffy. Slowly blend in pumpkin mixture. Refrigerate until ready to use.

CHOCOLATE GLAZE:

1/4 teaspoon vanilla extract
1 Tablespoon water
2/3 cup powdered sugar

1 Tablespoon butter
2 Tablespoons cocoa

In small saucepan over low heat, melt butter; add cocoa and water. Cook, stirring constantly, until mixture thickens. Do not boil. Remove from heat; gradually add powdered sugar and vanilla, beating with whisk until smooth. Add additional water, 1/2 teaspoon at a time, until of desired consistency. About 1/2 cup glaze.

Assemble:
Assemble cake by cutting cake crosswise into four equal pieces. Place one piece on serving plate; spread about 3/4 cup pumpkin filling over top. Repeat layering with remaining cake and filling, ending with cake layer. Spread chocolate glaze over top; garnish with almonds, if desired. Refrigerate until serving time. Refrigerate leftovers. Makes: 8 to 10 servings.

Chewy Oatmeal Raisin Pumpkin Cookies with Chocolate Chips

1-1/4 cup sifted flour
1-1/2 teaspoon salt
1 teaspoon baking powder
1/4 teaspoon soda
3/4 cup quick cooking rolled oats
1 cup brown sugar
3/4 cup granulated sugar
1/2 cup butter

1 teaspoon cinnamon
1/2 teaspoon nutmeg
1 egg
1 cup canned pumpkin
1 cup raisins
1 cup chopped nuts
1 cup chocolate chips

Sift first 4 ingredients together; add oats. Blend well the next 5 ingredients. Beat in egg. Gradually mix in dry ingredients and the pumpkin. Stir in remaining ingredients. Drop by rounded teaspoon on lightly greased cookie sheet. Bake in moderate oven 375 ° F for 14 to 16 minutes. Makes: 4 dozen.

Oatmeal Pumpkin Chocolate Chip Cookies

2 cups flour
1 cup quick oats
1 teaspoon baking soda
1 teaspoon cinnamon
1/2 teaspoon salt
1 cup butter

1 cup brown sugar, packed
1 cup granulated sugar
1 large egg, beaten
1 teaspoon vanilla
1 cup pumpkin puree
1 cup semisweet chocolate chips

Preheat oven to 350° F. Combine flour, oats, baking soda, cinnamon and salt. Set aside. Cream the butter. Gradually add sugars, beating until light and fluffy. Add egg and vanilla; mix well. Alternately add dry ingredients and pumpkin, mixing well after each. Stir in chocolate chips. For each cookie, drop 2 teaspoons dough for small cookies, 1/4 cup for large cookies, onto lightly greased cookie sheet Bake for 10 to 15 minutes for small cookies, 20 to 25 minutes for large cookies, or until cookies are firm and lightly browned. Remove from cookie sheets and cool on racks.

Pumpkin Nut Bars

1 cup cooked pumpkin puree
1/2 cup margarine, melted
2 egg whites, slightly beaten
2 cups oats

1 cup brown sugar, packed
1/2 cup shredded coconut, toasted
1/2 cup wheat germ
1 cup chopped salted peanuts

Preheat oven to 350° F. Using a large bowl; lightly beat egg whites; add pumpkin and melted margarine; beat until smooth. In another bowl combine oats, brown sugar, coconut, wheat germ, and nuts. Fold oat mixture into pumpkin mixture to form stiff dough. Press dough into a lightly greased 15-1/2 x 10-1/2 inch jellyroll pan. Bake 40 to 45 minutes or until golden brown. While warm, cut into 2 x 3 inch bars. Yield about 30 bars. Serve warm or cool completely.

Iced Pumpkin Cookies

1 cup unsalted butter
1 cup sugar
1 cup pureed pumpkin
1 egg
1 teaspoon vanilla extract
1 teaspoon baking powder
1/2 teaspoon salt

1 teaspoon cinnamon
1/2 teaspoon nutmeg
1 cup walnuts, coarsely chopped
1 cup raisins
2 cups all purpose flour
1/2 teaspoon baking soda

Preheat oven to 350° F. Cream butter and sugar until fluffy. Add pumpkin, egg and vanilla and mix well. Combine flour, baking powder, baking soda, salt, cinnamon and nutmeg. Stir into mixture until well blended. Add nuts and raisins. Drop by teaspoonful onto parchment covered baking sheet, about 2 inches apart. Bake 15 minutes, or until golden. Cool.

ICING:

2 cups sifted confectioner's sugar
3 Tablespoons orange juice or rum

1/4 cup butter, softened
1 teaspoon vanilla

Cream confectioner's sugar and butter. Add remaining ingredients and beat until smooth. Drizzle over cookies.

Spicy Pumpkin Cookies

1/4 cup margarine, softened
1/2 cup light brown sugar
1/2 cup pumpkin puree
1 egg
1 cup flour
1/2 cup raisins
1/2 cup chopped almonds

2 teaspoons baking powder
1 teaspoon cinnamon
1/4 teaspoon ginger
1/4 teaspoon nutmeg
1/4 teaspoon salt
1/4 cup diced,
Candied orange peel

Preheat oven to 350° F. Sift together flour, baking powder, cinnamon, ginger, nutmeg and salt and set aside. In a large mixing bowl, beat butter and sugar until fluffy. Beat in egg and pumpkin. Stir in flour mixture. Add in nuts, orange peel and raisins, mixing well. Drop rounded teaspoonful of dough onto a cookie sheet. Flatten slightly with spoon. Bake until done.

Pumpkin & Spice Raisin Cookies

2-1/2 cups flour
1/2 teaspoon baking soda
1/4 teaspoon salt
2 teaspoons pumpkin pie spice
1 cup dark brown sugar
1/2 cup sugar

3/4 cup butter, softened
1 large egg
1 cup pumpkin
1 teaspoon vanilla
1 cup raisins
1/2 cup chopped walnuts

Preheat oven 300° F. In medium size bowl, combine flour, soda, salt and pumpkin pie spice. Mix well with wire whisk. Set aside. In a large bowl blend sugars with mixer at medium speed. Add butter and beat to form a grainy paste. Scrape sides of bowl, then, add egg, pumpkin, and vanilla. Beat at medium speed until light and fluffy. Add flour mixture, raisins, and walnuts. Blend at low speed just until combined, being careful to not over mix. Drop by rounded spoonfuls on un-greased cookie sheets, 1-1/2 inch apart. Bake 22 to 24 minutes until cookies are slightly browned around edges. Immediately transfer cookies to a cool surface.

Pumpkin Macaroons

1 cup ground pecans
1/2 cup flour
1/2 teaspoon vanilla
1/4 cup unsweetened flaked coconut
1/2 teaspoon finely grated lemon peel

1 egg white
1/4 cup maple syrup
1/2 cup pumpkin puree

Combine pecans, flour, lemon peel, and coconut in a medium size bowl. Break egg white into a medium bowl and beat with mixer till soft peaks form. Gradually add syrup and vanilla, and fold into pecan mix, adding pumpkin as you go. Line cookie sheet with parchment paper; drop rounded teaspoonfuls onto it. Let relax at room temperature 30 minutes. Preheat oven to 300° F. Bake until just beginning to brown, 25 to 30 minutes. Let cool on a rack until completely cool. Store tightly covered.

Frosted Pumpkin Cookies

1 cup butter, softened
3/4 cup granulated sugar
3/4 cup brown sugar; packed
1 large egg
1 cup canned pumpkin
2 teaspoons vanilla
1 tub cream cheese frosting

3 cups flour
1/2 teaspoon baking soda
1-1/2 teaspoon baking powder
1 teaspoon ground cinnamon
1/2 teaspoon ground nutmeg
1-1/2 cup pecans, chopped

Heat oven to 350° F. In large mixer bowl, beat butter, sugar, and brown sugar until light and fluffy. Add egg; beat well. Add pumpkin and vanilla, then add dry ingredients; beat on low speed to combine. Stir in pecans except 1/2 cup to toast for garnish. Place dough by tablespoonfuls 2 inches apart on greased baking sheets. Bake for 10 to 12 minutes, or until golden brown. Cool on baking sheet for 2 min. Remove to wire rack to cool completely. Frost top of cookies with frosting! Garnish, with toasted pecans if desired. Yield: 5 dozen

Old Fashioned Soft Pumpkin Cookies

2-1/2 cups all-purpose flour
1 teaspoon baking soda
1 teaspoon baking powder
1 teaspoon ground cinnamon
1/2 teaspoon ground nutmeg
1/2 teaspoon salt

1-1/2 cup sugar
1/2 cup butter; softened
1 cup solid pack pumpkin
1 egg
1 teaspoon vanilla extract

Preheat oven to 350° F. Combine dry ingredients in a medium bowl. Cream sugar and butter in large mixer bowl until well blended then beat in pumpkin, egg and vanilla until smooth. Gradually add flour mixture. Drop by rounded tablespoons onto greased baking sheets. Bake, in oven for 15 to 18 minutes or until edges are firm. Cool on baking sheets for 2 minutes; remove to wire racks to cool completely. Drizzle glaze over cookies.

GLAZE:
2 cups sifted powdered sugar
3 Tablespoons milk

1 Tablespoon butter; melted
1 teaspoon vanilla extract

Combine powdered sugar, milk, melted butter and vanilla extract in small bowl until smooth.

Makes 3 dozen cookies.

Pumpkin Cookies

1 teaspoon baking soda
1 teaspoon baking powder
1 teaspoon cinnamon
1 cup rice flour
3/4 cup potato starch flour

1/2 cup shortening
3/4 cup sugar
1 teaspoon vanilla
1 cup pumpkin
1/2 cup nuts

Preheat oven to 350° F. Sift dry ingredients together. Cream shortening and sugar., add vanilla and pumpkin. Add dry ingredients and nuts. Beat until smooth. Shape cookies into 1 inch balls and place on a greased cookie sheet. Press flat with fork. Bake for 9 to 12 minutes.

Bran Pumpkin Spice Cookies

2 cups all purpose flour
1/2 cup cake flour
1 teaspoon baking soda
1 teaspoon baking powder
3/4 teaspoon salt
2 teaspoons cinnamon
3/4 teaspoon nutmeg
1/2 teaspoon ginger
1/4 teaspoon allspice
1/4 teaspoon cloves

8 Tablespoons butter, softened
8 Tablespoons shortening
1 cup light brown sugar
1 extra-large egg
1 extra-large egg yolk
1 Tablespoon. molasses
2 teaspoons vanilla extract
1 cup pumpkin puree
3/4 cup chopped dates or raisins
3 Tablespoons bran

Preheat oven to 375° F. Lightly grease and flour cookie sheets. Sift dry ingredients together. In separate bowl, cream butter, shortening and sugar, and beat for 1 minute. Beat in egg and egg yolk. Blend in molasses and vanilla. Add pumpkin and blend well. Blend in the sifted dry ingredients by hand, in two additions, beating just until the flour has been absorbed. Stir in the dates or raisins and bran.

Drop dough by rounded Tablespoons full, 2-1/2 inches apart, onto prepared sheets. Bake in middle of the oven for 12 to 14 minutes, or until firm to the touch. Transfer cookies to racks and cool 20 minutes. Store cookies in an airtight container.

Orange Pumpkin Walnut Cookies

FILLING

2 cups raisins   3/4 cup chopped walnuts
1/2 cup frozen orange juice, thawed

Process raisins, walnuts, and orange juice in food processor.

DOUGH

1 cup sugar   1 large egg
1 teaspoon vanilla   2 teaspoon baking powder
1 Tablespoon pumpkin pie spice   2-3/4 cup flour

Preheat oven to 375° F.

In a large bowl, cream butter and sugar with an electric mixer. Beat in egg and vanilla. Add baking powder, spice, and flour one cup at a time mixing after each addition. The dough will be very stiff; blend last cup of flour in by hand. Do not chill dough.

Divide dough into 2 balls. On a floured surface, roll each ball into a circle about 12 inches in diameter. Cut with any geometric shaped cookies cutters, dipping in flour before each use. Place half the cookies on cookie sheets. Place about 1 tablespoon filling on cookie. Top with another cookie and press to seal edges. Bake, for 12 to 15 minutes or until lightly browned.

Variations:
Replace filling with apricot jam. Use dates instead of raisins.

Pumpkin Cream Squares

COOKIE

3/4 cup butter
2 cups sugar
4 eggs, beaten
1 15 oz can pumpkin puree
2 cups all-purpose flour
2 teaspoons baking powder

1/2 teaspoon baking soda
1/2 teaspoon salt
1 teaspoon ground cinnamon
1/4 teaspoon ground nutmeg
1 cup chopped walnuts

CREAM FILLING

1 small package cream cheese
1/3 cup butter, softened

1 teaspoon vanilla extract
3 cups sifted confectioners' sugar

Preheat oven 350° F. Butter and flour a 10 x 15 inch jellyroll pan. In a large bowl, cream together 3/4 cup butter and sugar until light and fluffy. Beat eggs in one at a tune, then, stir in the pumpkin. Combine flour, baking powder, baking soda, salt, cinnamon, and nutmeg; stir into the pumpkin mixture. Stir in walnuts. Spread evenly onto pan. Bake for 30 to 35 minutes in the preheated oven, or until toothpick inserted near the center comes out clean. Cool completely before frosting.

In a medium bowl, mix together the cream cheese, 1/3 cup butter, and vanilla until smooth. Gradually blend in sugar, then, beat until smooth. Spread over cooled pumpkin bars. Cut into squares.

Pumpkin Squares

COOKIES CRUST

5 Tablespoons vegetable oil
1/3 cup honey

1 cup whole wheat pastry flour

FILLING

3-1/4 cups cooked pumpkin
1 cup cashew milk
1/4 cup corn starch
1/4 cup cashew butter
1/2 cup honey
1/2 cup maple syrup
1 teaspoon vanilla extract

2 teaspoons ground cinnamon
1 teaspoon ground coriander
1 teaspoon mace
1/4 teaspoon ground allspice
Dash ginger (optional)
1-1/2 Tablespoons molasses
Dash salt

Preheat oven to 425° F. Cookie crust: In a food processor, combine oil, honey, and flour. Process until blended by pulsing 20 to 30 seconds. Press crumbs into a 9 x 9 x 2 inch pan. Set aside.

Place the pumpkin and milk in a food processor. Puree, then, add remaining ingredients and process to a smooth, thick cream. Pour filling into crust. Bake for 15 minutes at 425° F. then reduce oven temperature to 250° F.; continue baking for 1-1/4 hours. Place on rack to cool and then refrigerate before cutting. When cold, squares will be firm.

Carrot-Pumpkin Bars with Orange Icing

2 cups all-purpose flour
2 teaspoons baking powder
1/4 cup milk
1 teaspoon vanilla
1 cup shredded carrots
1 cup chopped walnuts
Orange Icing walnut halves
1 teaspoon finely shredded orange peel

1 cup canned pumpkin
2/3 cup cooking oil
1/2 teaspoon baking soda
1/4 teaspoon salt
3 eggs, beaten
1-1/2 cups packed brown sugar

Preheat oven to 350° F. Grease a 15 x 10 x 1 inch baking pan; set aside. In a large mixing bowl stir together the flour, baking powder, orange peel, baking soda, and salt. Set flour mixture aside. In a medium bowl, combine eggs and brown sugar. Stir in pumpkin, oil, milk and vanilla. Stir in carrots and walnuts. Add egg mixture to flour mixture, stirring with a wooden spoon until combined. Spread batter into the prepared pan. Bake for 20 to 25 minutes or until a wooden toothpick inserted near the center comes out clean. Cool in pan on a wire rack. Spread with Orange Icing and cut into triangles or bars. If desired, garnish each with a walnut half. Store in an airtight container, in the refrigerator for up to 3 days. Makes: 36.

ORANGE ICING:
In a mixing bowl, combine 1-1/2 cups sifted powdered sugar and enough orange liqueur or orange juice (1 to 2 tablespoons) to make an icing with a consistency that is easy to drizzle.

More Deserts

Pumpkin Amaretto Cheesecake

1-1/2 cups graham cracker crumbs
1/4 cup sugar
1/3 cup butter, melted
16 oz. cream cheese,
1 cup light brown sugar, packed
2 cups pumpkin puree
2 egg yolks

4 egg whites
1-1/2 teaspoons cinnamon
1/2 teaspoon nutmeg
2 Tablespoons flour
2 Tablespoons whipping cream
2 Tablespoons Amaretto

Preheat oven to 325° F. In a 9 inch spring form pan, mix graham cracker crumbs, sugar and melted butter. Press mixture evenly onto the bottom and sides of pan. Bake 8 minutes. Remove from oven and cool, in a large bowl, using electric mixer, whip cream cheese until smooth. Stir in brown sugar, blending until thoroughly mixed. Add pumpkin. Add egg yolks one at a time, blending after each until smooth. Add 2 egg whites at a time, blending well. Blend cinnamon, nutmeg, flour, Amaretto and whipping cream. Pour mixture into prepared crust. Set pan in a large roasting pan and fill with 1/2 inch tap water. Bake 1 hour, or until knife inserted in center comes out clean. Remove from oven, chill 6 to 8 hours in the refrigerator.

Maple-Pumpkin Cheesecake

Graham cracker crust in 8 inch spring form pie pan

1 lb low-fat cottage cheese
1/2 cup plain yogurt
3/4 cup pumpkin puree
1/4 cup flour

3 eggs
1 teaspoon vanilla
1/4 cup maple syrup
1/2 teaspoon pumpkin pie spice

Preheat oven to 325° F. Put all ingredients into blender, a little at a time, alternating wet and dry. Process until smooth, then pour into crust and spread evenly. Bake for about 50 minutes. Let cool before serving. May be topped with yogurt, flavored with 2 tablespoons maple syrup.

Pumpkin Cheesecake

FILLING:

8 ounces cream cheese
1 egg
1 Tablespoon corn starch

1/3 cup sugar
1/4 cup canned pumpkin

In a mixing bowl, beat ingredients until very smooth. Set aside and prepare cake batter. Pour into glass dish on top of batter as described in cake instructions below.

CAKE:

2 sticks butter
3 eggs
2-1/2 cups flour
1 cup sugar
1-1/2 teaspoon vanilla
1/2 cup sour cream

3/4 teaspoon salt
1/2 teaspoon baking soda
1/3 teaspoon (or less) salt
2 teaspoons baking powder
1 teaspoon cinnamon
1/2 cup pumpkin, pureed

Preheat oven to 350° F. In a large bowl cream butter, sugar and vanilla until light and fluffy. Add eggs and beat well. Add flour, baking powder, baking soda, cinnamon and salt. Mix in pumpkin and sour cream. Blend thoroughly until smooth. Pour 1/2 of batter into a buttered 13 x 9 inch glass baking dish. Add the filling mix, spreading the batter evenly in the dish. Add remaining batter and lightly swirl into filling. Bake for 50 to 55 minutes. Allow to cool. Cut into twelve servings

Pineapple Pumpkin Cheesecake

1-1/2 cups packed brown sugar
12 ounces cream cheese
1 can (16 oz.) pumpkin
4 eggs

2 Tablespoons flour
4 teaspoons pumpkin pie spice
1 teaspoon vanilla extract

Preheat oven to 350° F. Place a 9 x 13 inch pan in hot water on lower rack in oven. Set aside 2 tablespoons of brown sugar. In food processor, combine remaining sugar with cream cheese. Process 20 seconds, add pumpkin, eggs, flour, spice and vanilla extract. Process, 10 seconds, scraping sides once. Pour batter into 8 inch spring form pan coated with cooking spray. Bake 50 minutes, then turn oven off and let stand 1 hour. Do not open oven door. Run knife around sides of pan and refrigerate 3 hours before removing.

TOPPING:
1 can sliced pineapple in heavy syrup

Drain pineapple, reserving syrup. Cook reserved syrup, reserved sugar and diced pineapple over medium high heat until thick, without stirring. Just before serving, arrange pineapple on top of cheesecake. Drizzle with glaze.

Pumpkin Pizza

1 8 oz package cream cheese
1 can solid pack pumpkin
1 teaspoon grated orange peel

2 7 oz jars marshmallow cream
1 teaspoon ground cinnamon

In a mixing bowl, beat the cream cheese and marshmallow cream until smooth. Stir in pumpkin, cinnamon and orange peel. Spread a thin layer over a pizza crust. Sprinkle the top with cinnamon sugar, and bake!

Pumpkin Swirl Cheesecake

2 cups vanilla wafer crumbs
1 teaspoon vanilla
1/4 cup margarine, melted
3 eggs
16 oz Neufchatel Cheese, softened

1 cup canned pumpkin
3/4 teaspoon cinnamon
1/4 teaspoon ground nutmeg
3/4 cup sugar

Combine crumbs and margarine; press into bottom and sides of 9 inch spring form pan. Combine Neufchatel cheese, 1/2 cup sugar, and vanilla, mixing at medium speed on electric mixer until well blended. Add eggs, one at a time, mixing well after each. Remove 1 cup Neufchatel Cheese mixture and set aside, then add pumpkin, 1/4 cup sugar and spices to remaining Neufchatel cheese mixture, mixing well. Layer half pumpkin mixture and half Neufchatel cheese mixture over crust; repeat layers. Cut through batter with knife several times for marble effect. Bake at 350° F. 55 minutes. Loosen cake from rim of pan; cool before removing rim of pan. Chill.

Pumpkin Rum Mousse

1 cup canned pumpkin
1 envelope unflavored gelatin
2/3 cups sugar
4 eggs
1/4 cup rum
1/2 teaspoon cinnamon

1/2 teaspoon ginger
1/4 teaspoon mace
1/4 teaspoon ground cloves
1 cup heavy whipped cream
Nuts-almonds

Warm rum in a small saucepan! Slowly add in gelatin, stirring constantly. Heat and stir until gelatin is completely dissolved. Set aside and cool slightly. Beat eggs in a large mixing bowl. Gradually add sugar to the eggs beating for 3 to 4 minutes until it is thick and light. In a second bowl, combine pumpkin, cloves, ginger, cinnamon, and mace. Combine rum, gelatin and egg mixtures, stirring well. Gently pour in the heavy cream. Pour Mousse into small serving dishes. Refrigerate for several hours until firm. Decorate with whipped Cream and nuts.

Pumpkin-Eggnog Cheesecake

CRUST

20 gingersnaps

1/4 cup sugar

2 Tablespoons butter, melted

1/2 cup walnuts

CHEESECAKE

4 large eggs, separated

3/4 cups sugar

16 oz can pumpkin

16 oz cream cheese, softened

1/8 teaspoon ground cloves

1 teaspoon ground cinnamon

1/2 teaspoon ground allspice

1/2 teaspoon ground ginger

1/2 teaspoon ground nutmeg

Walnuts for garnish

TOPPING

1 Tablespoon cornstarch

1/8 teaspoon ground nutmeg

1 cup prepared eggnog

Preheat oven to 350° F. Spray 9 x 3 inch spring form pan with nonstick cooking spray. In food processor grind gingersnaps, walnuts, and sugar until finely ground; stir in butter. Press mixture onto bottom and 2-1/2 inches up sides of pan; set aside. In a small bowl, with mixer at high speed, beat egg whites until foamy. Gradually beat in sugar until soft peaks form; set aside. In a large bowl, with same beaters and with mixer at medium speed, beat egg yolks, pumpkin, cream cheese, cinnamon, allspice, ginger, cloves, and nutmeg until well blended. Fold egg white mixture into cream cheese mixture; pour in pan and bake 1 hour or until knife inserted comes out clean. Cool in pan on a wire rack.

In a small saucepan, mix eggnog, cornstarch, and nutmeg, cooking over medium heat; bring to a boil. Reduce heat to low; simmer until mixture thickens. Let stand 10 minutes to cool slightly. Remove side of spring form pan from cheesecake and spread eggnog mixture over cheesecake. Garnish with walnuts. Refrigerate cheesecake at least 4 hours.

Pumpkin Cognac Cheesecake

CRUST

1-1/2 cup graham cracker crumbs
1/4 cup almonds, ground
2 Tablespoons sugar

1/2 teaspoon ginger, ground
1/2 teaspoon cinnamon
6 Tablespoons butter, melted

FILLING

2 lbs. cream cheese, softened
1-1/4 cup sugar
3 Tablespoons cognac
3 Tablespoons maple syrup
1 teaspoon ground ginger

1 teaspoon cinnamon
1/2 teaspoon nutmeg
4 large eggs room temperature
1/4 cup heavy cream
1 cup canned pumpkin

TOPPING

1 Tablespoon cognac
1 Tablespoon maple syrup
1/2 cup sliced almonds, toasted

1-1/2 cup sour cream
3 Tablespoons sugar

Generously grease a 10 inch spring form pan. To prepare the crust, thoroughly combine crumbs, almonds, sugar, ginger, cinnamon, and melted butter. Press firmly into bottom of the pan. Set aside. Heat oven to 250° F.

Beat cream cheese until smooth in mixer. Gradually add sugar, beating until light and fluffy. Add cognac, maple syrup, ginger, cinnamon and nutmeg. Blend well. Add eggs one at a time, beating well after each addition. Add cream and pumpkin. Mix well. Pour filling into unbaked crust, and smooth the top. Bake for two hours, until soft but firm. Shake pan slightly. Cake should not wiggle. Remove and let cool on a rack for 30 minutes. After 20 minutes, heat oven to 350° F. To prepare topping, combine sour cream, sugar, cognac and maple syrup. Mix thoroughly. Spread topping on cooled cheesecake. Return assembled cheesecake to oven for 7 minutes. Remove and let cheesecake cool on a rack for 4 hours at room temperature before removing sides of pan. Garnish outer edge of cake with toasted almond slices.

Pumpkin Mousse with Vanilla Sauce

1 Tablespoon gelatin
2 Tablespoons cold water
3 egg yolks
1/3 cup + 1 Tablespoon sugar
1 cup heavy cream, whipped

1-1/4 cup pumpkin
1 teaspoon cinnamon
1 teaspoon nutmeg
1 teaspoon allspice

To a small bowl, sprinkle gelatin over cold water. Place bowl in simmering water; stir until gelatin is dissolved. Beat egg yolks with sugar. Stir in pumpkin, cinnamon, nutmeg, allspice, and dissolved gelatin. Fold whipped cream into pumpkin mixture. Pour mousse in mold and chill thoroughly. Serve with vanilla sauce.

Sauce:
Scald milk and light cream with vanilla. In double boiler, beat egg yolks, sugar, and a pinch of salt. Gradually beat in hot milk mixture. Cook sauce over hot water, stirring constantly until it thickens and coats a spoon. Chill!

Pumpkin Flan

1 cup pumpkin
1/4 cup honey
3/4 teaspoon Cinnamon
5 eggs

1 can evaporated milk
1 teaspoon Vanilla extract
1 Tablespoon Brandy, optional
1/4 cup Brown sugar, packed

Combine pumpkin, honey and cinnamon. Beat the eggs, add milk, vanilla and pumpkin mixture to the eggs. Stir in brandy, mixing well. Sprinkle brown sugar over the bottom of a buttered 10 inch baking dish or six individual custard cups. Very slowly, pour in the custard mixture and place in a pan of hot water. Bake at 350° F. for one hour, or 325° F. for 45 minutes for cups, until the custard is set. Insert a knife into the custard. If it comes out clean, the custard is done. Cover and chill for 2 to 4 hours before serving. For a pumpkin flan "brulee" sprinkle brown sugar over baked custard and broil about 4 inches from the heat until sugar bubbles, watching because it burns very easily. When the sugar bubbles, remove it immediately, cover and chill

Pumpkin Mousse

10 oz canned pumpkin
1/2 cup sour cream
1/2 cup cream cheese
1 cup sugar
1/2 Tablespoon salt

2 Tablespoons pumpkin pie spice
1 Tablespoon ground ginger
2 egg yolks
1-1/2 cup whipping cream
2 egg whites

GARNISH
Crystallized ginger finely chopped

In a large stainless-steel bowl over a hot-water bath, combine pumpkin, sour cream, cream cheese, 1 cup sugar, salt, pumpkin pie spice, and ginger. Heat water to boiling, beating mixture with mixer until ingredients are fluffy. Add egg yolks and beat for 3 minutes. Remove mixture from heat and refrigerate for 10 minutes. Meanwhile, whip cream with 2 tablespoons sugar, fold the whipping cream (reserving 1/3 for garnish) into chilled pumpkin mixture, then carefully fold in egg whites. Chill for 4-6 hours. Top with remaining whipped cream and finely chopped crystallized ginger.

Serves 4 to 6

Holiday Pumpkin Dip

2 cups pumpkin puree
1 cup dark brown sugar 1 package
1/2 teaspoon grated nutmeg
8 oz. cream cheese, room temperature

1/2 teaspoon ground ginger
2 teaspoons ground cinnamon

Cream pumpkin and cream cheese together. Add in all other ingredients, stirring until well mixed. Refrigerate overnight. Serve with ginger snaps and graham crackers.

Rich Chocolate Pumpkin Truffles

2-1/2 cups vanilla wafers, crushed
1 cup almonds, toasted and ground
1/2 cup powdered sugar, sifted
2 teaspoons cinnamon

6 oz. chocolate chips
1/2 cup pumpkin, canned
1/3 cup coffee liqueur
1/4 cup powdered sugar

Note: Apple juice may be substituted for coffee liqueur if desired. In bowl, combine vanilla wafer crumbs, ground almonds, the 1/2 cup powdered sugar, and cinnamon. Blend in chocolate, pumpkin, and coffee liqueur. Form into 1- inch balls. Chill. Dust with remaining powdered sugar just before serving.

Pudding with Ginger Cream

3 eggs
1-1/4 cups sugar
1-1/2 teaspoons cinnamon
1-/2 teaspoons nutmeg
1/4 cup margarine, melted

1-1/2 teaspoons vanilla
1-3/4 cups dry bread crumbs
2 cups milk
1 cup canned pumpkin
1/2 cup raisins

GINGER CREAM
1 cup whipping cream
1/2 teaspoon ginger

3 Tablespoons sugar

Heat oven to 350° F. Spray 8 or 9 inch square pan with nonstick cooking spray, in large bowl, beat eggs until well blended. Add 1-1/4 cups sugar, cinnamon, nutmeg, margarine and vanilla; beat well. Add bread crumbs, milk and pumpkin; mix well. Let stand 10 minutes. Add raisins to batter; mix well. Spread evenly in the prepared pan. Bake at 350° F. for 37 to 47 minutes or until knife inserted 1-1/2 inches from edge comes out clean. Cool 30 minutes, to small bowl, beat whipping cream, gradually adding 3 tablespoons sugar and ginger until soft peaks form. To serve, cut pudding into squares. Serve warm or cool topped with ginger cream. Keep stored in refrigerator.

Pumpkin Seed Brittle

1 cup sugar
1-1/2 teaspoons margarine
2 cups pumpkin seeds hulled and toasted

1/2 teaspoon vanilla extract

Lightly grease a cookie sheet. in a large saucepan stir sugar over medium low heat 8-10 minutes until melted and dark golden brown; sugar will look crumbly before melting. Take from hcat; stir in remaining ingredients. Immediately pour onto buttered cookie sheet with a wide metal spatula and press out mixture to 1/3 inch thickness. Let cool and harden. Break into bite size pieces. Store in an air-tight container with wax paper between layers. Store room temperature. Keeps, 6 weeks.

Pumpkin Fudge

2 cups granulated sugar
1/4 teaspoon cornstarch
1/2 cup evaporated milk
2 Tablespoons pumpkin

1/4 teaspoon pumpkin pie spice
1/2 teaspoon vanilla extract
1 cup chopped nuts

In a 2-quart saucepan, cook sugar, pumpkin, spice, cornstarch and milk, stirring frequently, until mixture reaches 234° F, or it forms a soft ball in a little cold water. Add vanilla and nuts and cool in a pan of ice water to 110° F. Beat until fudge loses its gloss. Pour into a lightly buttered 8 x 8 x 2 inch pan and cool. Score and cut when almost cold. Store in wax paper lined metal can. Fudge will keep for several weeks.

Pumpkin Jam

1 medium pumpkin
4 lb bag sugar

4 lemons
4 oranges

Cut up and dice pumpkin. Cut up 4 lemons and 4 oranges. Combine pumpkin, lemon and orange and cover with the sugar. Use 2 bowls if necessary. Let stand over night, covered. Next day, mix well and cook until pumpkin is clear. Pack in sterile jars and seal immediately.

Pumpkin Walnut Fudge

4 cups sugar
1 cup milk
3 teaspoons light corn syrup
1 cup pumpkin puree or canned puree

3 teaspoons butter
1 teaspoon vanilla
2 cups walnuts, chopped

In a 4-quart heavy saucepan, combine sugar, milk, corn syrup, pumpkin and a pinch of salt. Cook over moderate heat, stirring, until the sugar is dissolved, then, let cook undisturbed, until a candy thermometer registers 238° F. Remove pan from heat,, add the butter, (do not stir it into the mixture), and let cool until it is 140° F. Stir in the vanilla and walnuts, beat with a wooden spoon for 30 seconds to a minute, or until it begins to loose its gloss. Immediately pour into a buttered 9 inch square pan. Let fudge cool until it begins to harden. Cut into squares and let cool completely. Makes about 2 pounds.

White Chocolate Pumpkin Fudge

3 cups milk
5 cups pumpkin
7 teaspoons pumpkin pie spice
3 cups granulated sugar
1/2 cup butter or margarine

1 cup chopped nuts
1 cup marshmallow cream
8 oz white chocolate
1 teaspoon vanilla
Dash salt

Combine the milk, pumpkin, spice, salt, butter and nuts in a 5-quart saucepan and bring to a boil, cooking until the mixture reaches the firm ball stage. Then, stir in marshmallow cream, white chocolate and vanilla. Stir until it starts to get thick. Pour into a buttered pan; let set. Cut into squares.

Pumpkin Pudding with Praline Sauce & Vanilla-Rum Creme Fraiche

PUDDING:

3 cups pumpkin puree
1/2 cup sugar
2 Tablespoons orange juice
1/4 teaspoon cinnamon
4 each egg yolks
1/4 cup Butter

1 Tablespoon flour
1/4 cup crystallized ginger
2 each egg whites
1/4 cup sugar
1/2 cup pecans, chopped

Preheat the oven to 400° F. In a small saucepan, heat the puree, sugar, orange juice and cinnamon. Cook gently for five minutes. Remove from the heat and whisk in butter, egg yolks, flour and ginger. Cool. Whip egg whites with the sugar until stiff peak. Fold whipped whites into pumpkin mixture. Fill 4 inch ramekins full and sprinkle with sugar and pecans. Bake for 20 to 25 minutes. Serve hot.

SAUCE:

1 lb. dark brown sugar
1-1/4 cup light corn syrup
4 oz. butter

1 teaspoon salt
2 cups cream
1 teaspoon vanilla extract

In a saucepan, slowly bring brown sugar, corn syrup, butter and salt to a boil. Remove from the heat, add cream and vanilla.

CREME FRAICHE:

2 cups crème fraiche
1 Tablespoon sugar

1/2 vanilla bean, seed only
2 Tablespoon rum

Combine all ingredients and whip to soft peaks. Serve the puddings while still warm with two tablespoon of the sauce over the top followed by a heaping tablespoon of the whipped crème fraiche.

116

Pumpkin Ice Cream 1

SWEET CREAM BASE:

2 cups heavy cream	2 eggs
1 cup milk	3/4 cup sugar

Whisk eggs in mixing bowl. Whisk in the sugar, a little at a time until completely blended. Whisk *in* cream. Whisk in milk.

ICE CREAM:

Sweet Cream Base	1 teaspoon cinnamon
1 cup canned pumpkin	1 teaspoon nutmeg

Pour 1/2 of Sweet Cream Base into a second bowl. Mix in the pumpkin thoroughly. Stir in cinnamon and nutmeg. Add remaining Sweet Cream Base. Place mixture into ice cream maker. Follow the manufacturer's instructions and freeze.

Pumpkin Ice Cream 2

5-1/3 oz Evaporated milk	1/4 teaspoon nutmeg
2 eggs, separated	1 cup pumpkin puree
1/2 cup light brown sugar	1/8 teaspoon salt
1/4 teaspoon ginger	1/8 teaspoon cream of tartar
1/2 teaspoon cinnamon	

Combine evaporated milk, egg yolks, brown sugar, and spices in top of double boiler. Using a wire whisk beat the ingredients until smooth. Cook over simmering water until custard thickens, stirring constantly. Remove from heat. Stir in 1 cup pumpkin puree. Set aside. In medium-sized bowl beat egg whites, salt, and cream of tartar until stiff peaks are formed. Fold beaten egg whites into pumpkin custard. Scrape into freezer container or serving dish, cover tightly, and freeze until firm (about 3 hours). Serve directly from freezer.

Pumpkin Ice Cream Tarts

2 cups heavy cream
2 cups milk
1-1/4 cups brown sugar
1/4 teaspoon salt
4 egg yolks

2 cups pumpkin puree
1/4 teaspoon ground mace
1 teaspoon ground nutmeg
1/4 teaspoon ground cloves
1/4 teaspoon ground ginger

8 pre-baked pastry tart shells, each 2-1/2 to 3 inches in diameter 1/2 cup chopped walnuts or pecans, whipped cream, garnish

Combine cream, milk, sugar and salt in a heavy-bottom saucepan. Bring to a boil over medium-high heat, stirring often, until sugar has dissolved. Whisk egg yolks in a bowl until they turn lemon-yellow. Slowly whisk about 1 cup of the hot milk mixture into yolks. Then whisk yolk mixture into hot milk mixture. Continue to cook, stirring constantly, until custard thickens enough to coat the back of a spoon. Remove from heat; cool to lukewarm. Put pumpkin puree in a bowl, and whisk about 1 cup of the warm custard into the pumpkin. Whisk all the pumpkin mixture and the spices into the warm custard. Freeze in an ice-cream maker according to manufacturer's directions. To serve, scoop the ice cream into the pastry shells; top with whipped cream and nuts, if desired. Yields: 8 tarts.

Pumpkin Marmalade

2 cups sugar
2 oz. raisin, soaked in water
5 cups fresh pumpkin

1 lemon peel grated
kirsch or Maraschino liqueur

Layer peeled and sliced pumpkin in a pan, covering each layer with sugar. Let sit in refrigerator for 24 hours then cook for 2 hours on a low flame. A few minutes before cooking time is up, add the raisins that have been softened in water, lemon zest and 1 glass of Kirsch or Maraschino, according to preference. Put the hot marmalade in the canning jars and process to preserve.

Pickled Pumpkin Balls

2 cups pumpkin balls	1 cinnamon stick, broken
1-1/3 cups sugar	6 cloves
3/4 cup cider vinegar	6 whole allspice
1/2 cup water	4 2 inch strips lemon peel

Using a 1 inch melon-bailer, scoop out enough balls from the flesh of a pumpkin, to measure 2 cups. In a saucepan, combine sugar, cider vinegar, water, cinnamon stick, broken into pieces, cloves, whole allspice, and lemon peel. Bring the liquid to a boil over moderate heat, stirring and washing down any sugar crystals clinging to the sides of the pan with a brush dipped in cold water until sugar is dissolved. Cook syrup undisturbed for 5 minutes. Add the pumpkin balls; simmer for 15 minutes. Transfer the balls with a slotted spoon to a 1-pint jar. Reduce the syrup over high heat to 1 cup and pour it and the spices over the balls, allowing the mixture to cool. Chill for at least 3 hours. Transfer the pickles to a small serving bowl. Keep covered and chilled, for 1 week

Pumpkin-n-Fruit Jam

5 lbs pumpkin (fresh or canned)	5 cups sugar
1 lb dried apricots	2 Tablespoons lemon juice
1 lb seedless raisins	2 Tablespoons chopped
crystallized ginger	

For fresh pumpkin, peel, remove seeds, and cut into cubes. Cook pumpkin, mash and sieve. Mix in sugar and let stand for 12 hours. Wash and cut apricots, into pieces the size of raisins and add to the pumpkin. Add raisins, lemon juice, and ginger. Cook slowly until the mixture is thick. Seal and process in boiling water bath 10 minutes.

Pumpkin Apple Butter

1-3/4 cups pumpkin puree
1 cup apple juice
1 cup peeled and grated apple

1/2 cup packed brown sugar
3/4 teaspoon pumpkin pie spice

Combine pumpkin, apple juice, apple, sugar and pumpkin pie spice in medium saucepan. Bring to a boil. Reduce heat to low; simmer for 1-1/2 hours, stirring occasionally. Pour into container. Cover and chill. May be stored in refrigerator for up to two months.

Honey-Pumpkin Butter

2 cups cooked pumpkin, pureed
1/2 cup honey
1 teaspoon grated lemon rind
1 Tablespoon lemon juice
1/4 teaspoon salt

1/4 teaspoon nutmeg
1/4 teaspoon ginger
1 teaspoon cinnamon
1/8 teaspoon cloves

Mix all ingredients thoroughly. Simmer uncovered on low heat, about 40 minutes, stirring frequently, until thick. When it is thick enough for you, ladle into jars and refrigerate.

Pumpkin Butter

3 cups mashed pumpkin
2 cups sugar
1/2 teaspoon ground cinnamon

1/4 teaspoon ground cloves
1/2 teaspoon lemon juice

Combine all ingredients in a medium saucepan; stir well. Bring to a boil then reduce heat and simmer uncovered for 30 minutes until mixture is smooth and thickened. Quickly pour pumpkin butter mixture into hot jars, filling to 1/4 inch from top. Wipe jar rims clean. Cover at once with metal lids and screw-on bands. Process in a boiling water bath, 15 minutes.

Early American Pumpkin Butter

6 cups cooked pumpkin puree
2 cups pure maple syrup
2 cups light corn syrup
2 cups packed brown sugar
2 teaspoon lemon juice
1 teaspoon ground cinnamon

1 teaspoon nutmeg
1/2 teaspoon ground ginger
1/4 teaspoon ground cloves
1/4 teaspoon ground mace
1/4 teaspoon vanilla

Put the pumpkin in a large non-aluminum pot; stir in the maple syrup and corn syrup. When these are thoroughly combined, add the remaining ingredients. Set the pot over medium-high heat. When it begins to boil, partially cover it; mixture will splash profusely. Cook at a slow boil, stirring frequently to prevent sticking, until it thickens and turns a darker color, about 45 minutes. Ladle butter into hot jars leaving 1/4 inch head-space. Wipe rim with a clean damp cloth. Adjust lids and process in a boiling water bath for 15 minutes. Makes: 5 pints.

Pumpkin Butter

1 small lemon
1 16 oz. can solid-pack pumpkin
1/2 cup apple juice
1/2 cup brown sugar

1/2 teaspoon salt
1/4 teaspoon ginger
1/8 teaspoon cinnamon
1/8 teaspoon allspice

About 4 hours before serving or a day ahead: Grate lemon to make 1 teaspoon peel; squeeze to make 1 teaspoon juice. In a 2-quart saucepan over medium-high heat, heat lemon peel and juice and remaining ingredients to boiling. Reduce heat to medium-low, cook 30 minutes, stirring often. Spoon pumpkin mixture into a small bowl; cover & refrigerate until well chilled, at least 3 hours. Serve with warm biscuits.

Spiced Pumpkin & Pecan Butter

Zest of 1/2 orange
Zest of 1/2 lemon
3-1/2 cups pumpkin puree
2 cups light brown sugar, packed
3 Tablespoons orange juice
3 Tablespoons lemon juice

1-1/2 teaspoon cinnamon
1/2 teaspoon salt
1/4 teaspoon ground allspice
1/4 teaspoon ground ginger
Pinch of ground cloves
1/3 cup pecans, lightly toasted
and very finely chopped

Simmer the orange and lemon zest in 2 cups water in a saucepan for 10 minutes, then drain and mince it to a fine pulp. Measure out 1 tablespoon and reserve.

Combine in a heavy bottomed stainless steel or other non-reactive saucepan, the pumpkin, (add 1/2 cup water if you use canned pumpkin) orange zest, lemon zest, sugar, orange juice, lemon juice, cinnamon, salt, allspice, ginger and cloves. Bring to a boil over medium-high heat, stirring constantly. Lower the heat and simmer mixture, stirring often with a wooden spatula, until it has become very thick, about 15 minutes.

Sample the butter and make any adjustments to your taste at this point. Stir in the pecans and continue to cook for another 2 to 3 minutes.
Ladle the boiling-hot pumpkin butter into clean, hot half-pint canning jars, leaving 1/4-inch headspace. Seal the jars with new 2 piece, canning lids according to manufacturer's instructions. Process the jars for 10 minutes in a boiling water bath. Cool, label, and store for up to a year in a cool cupboard. Makes: 5 cups.

Beverages

Pink Lady Punch

4 cups cranberry juice
1-1/2 cup sugar

4 cups pineapple juice
2 quart ginger ale, chilled

Add all ingredients (chilled). Gently stir and serve. For a harvest presentation, serve in a chilled, hallowed out pumpkin shell.

Great Pumpkin Punch

1 Part Apple Cider
2 Parts Ginger Ale

1 Part Bacardi Rum

Serve in a hollowed-out pumpkin with little chunks of floating pumpkin.

Pumpkin Frappe

1/4 cup canned pumpkin
1/2 teaspoon cinnamon
2 scoops vanilla soy protein powder
3/4 cup frozen apple juice concentrate, undiluted

1/4 cup low-fat soy milk
1/8 teaspoon nutmeg
3 ice cubes

Combine ingredients in blender. Cover and blend at high speed about one minute. Serves: 2

Pumpkin Smoothie

1 can pumpkin, chilled
1 can evaporated milk, chilled
1/2 cup packed brown sugar
1/2 cup orange slices

1 cup orange juice, chilled
1/2 large banana, sliced
Ice cubes
Ground nutmeg or cinnamon

In blender, combine pumpkin, evaporated milk, orange juice, banana and sugar. Cover and blend until smooth. Serve over ice cubes; sprinkle with nutmeg or cinnamon and garnish with orange slices. Serves 6

126

Just
Pumpkin Pies
But Not
Just Any
Old Pumpkin Pie

Redused Fat Pumpkin Pie

2 eggs, slightly beaten
1 cup pumpkin puree
1 cup firmly packed brown sugar
1-1/2 teaspoon grown cinnamon
1/2 teaspoon salt

1/2 teaspoon ground nutmeg
2 Tablespoons melted butter
1 cup skim milk
1 teaspoon vanilla extract

Preheat oven to 425° F.
One 9-inch unbaked pie shell

In a large bowl, add filling ingredients in order given. Mix well with electric mixer or by hand. Pour into pie shell. Bake 15 minutes. Then reduce oven temperature to 350° F and continue baking for an additional 45 minutes or until knife inserted near the center comes out clean. Cool slightly and serve warm or chilled. Makes: one 9-inch pie.

Pumpkin Pie with Sass

One 9-inch unbaked pie shell
1-12 oz. can evaporated milk
1/2 teaspoon ground nutmeg
1/2 teaspoon ground ginger
1-1/2 teaspoons ground cinnamon
2 teaspoons TABASCO brand Pepper Sauce

1 16-oz. can pumpkin
2 large eggs
3/4 cup packed brown sugar
Whipped Cream
1/4 cup chopped pecans

Preheat oven to 400° F.

In large bowl, combine pumpkin, evaporated milk, eggs, brown sugar, TABASCO® Pepper Sauce, cinnamon, nutmeg and ginger. With electric mixer at medium speed, beat ingredients until well mixed. Pour mixture into prepared crust. Bake 40 to 45 minutes until knife inserted 1-inch from edge comes out clean. Cool pie wire rack. To serve, top pie whipped cream; garnish with chopped pecans.

In early colonial times, pumpkins were used as an ingredient for the crust of pies, not the filling.

Almond Pumpkin Pie

2 cups or 16 oz Pumpkin
14 oz Sweetened condensed milk
2 eggs
1 cup almonds, toasted and finely-chopped
1/2 teaspoon ground cinnamon
6 oz almond brickle chips
1 teaspoon almond extract

Preheat oven to 425° F. 1 (9-in) unbaked pastry shell. In large mixing bowl, combine all ingredients except brickle chips; mix well. Stir in 1/2 cup brickle chips. Pour into pastry shell. Top with remaining brickle chips.

Bake 15 minutes. Reduce oven temperature to 350°, bake 30 minutes longer or until knife inserted near center comes out clean.

Super Quick & E-Z Sugar Free Pumpkin Pie (No-Bake)

1 (16 oz.) can pumpkin
1 teaspoon cinnamon
2 small pkgs. sugar free vanilla pudding
1/2 teaspoon ginger
1/4 teaspoon cloves

Blend all ingredients together with a mixer. Pour into a pre cooked pie crust. Chill several hours before serving.

Pumpkin Gingersnap Pie

3-1/2 oz whipped topping
1 cup each: pecans and gingersnaps
1-1/2 Tablespoons pumpkin pie spice
1-1/2 cup half and half cream or milk
1 package vanilla instant pudding
1/2 cup canned pumpkin
1 graham cracker crumb crust

Beat half and half cream and pie filling in a large mixing bowl with a wire whisk for 1 minute. Let stand 5 minutes. Fold in topping and remaining ingredients; spoon into crust. Freeze until firm. Let stand at room temperature for 10 minutes before serving to soften. Store any leftovers in freezer.

No-Bake Double Layer Pumpkin Pie

1 (16 oz) can of pumpkin pie filling
1 Tablespoon sugar
1/2 teaspoon ground ginger
1 teaspoon ground cloves
4 ounces of cream cheese, softened
2 small packages of vanilla instant pudding
1-1/2 cups thawed whipped cream topping

1 Tablespoon half and half
1 teaspoon ground cinnamon
1 graham cracker crust
1 cup cold milk or half and half

Beat cream cheese, half and half and sugar with wire whisk until smooth. Gently stir in the whipped cream topping. Spread on bottom of graham cracker crust. Refrigerate for 30 minutes, in a bowl, pour milk, add pudding mix. Beat with wire whisk for one to two minutes; mixture will be thick. Stir in pumpkin and spices with wire whisk. Mix well. Spread over cream cheese layer. Refrigerate four hours, or until set.

Ginger-Snappy Pumpkin Pie (No-Bake)

20 ginger snap cookies
1 can pumpkin pie mix

2 cup whipped topping
1/4 cup crush peanut brittle

Cover bottom and sides of greased 9 inch pie pan with whole gingersnap cookies and place in freezer, in a mixing bowl gently stir together the pumpkin and whipped topping until thoroughly combined. Pour over frozen cookie shell and sprinkle with peanut brittle Freeze 4 hours or over night Remove from freezer 30 to 40 min before serving. Top with whipped cream and cinnamon

Pumpkins contain potassium and Vitamin A.

Creamy Pumpkin Pie (No-Bake)

1 cup canned pumpkin
1/2 cup cold milk
1 graham cracker pie crust
1 package vanilla flavor instant pudding and pie filling

1 teaspoon pumpkin pie spice
3-1/2 cups thawed Cool Whip

Combine pumpkin, milk, pudding mix and pumpkin pie spice in small mixer bowl. Blend with wire whisk or electric mixer (low speed) for one minute. Fold in 2-1/2 cups of the whipped topping. Spoon into crust. Freeze until firm, about 4 hours. Top with remaining whipped topping.

Pumpkin Pecan Pie

3 slightly beaten eggs
1 cup canned pumpkin
1 cup sugar 1 pastry shell
1/2 cup dark corn syrup

1/2 teaspoon cinnamon
1/4 teaspoon salt
1 cup pecans, chopped
1 teaspoon vanilla

Combine all ingredients except pecans. Pour into unbaked pastry shell. Top with pecans. Bake at 350° F. for 40 minutes.

Layered Mince & Pumpkin Pie

1-1/2 cups canned mincemeat
1 egg, beaten
1 cup pumpkin puree
1/2 cup white sugar

1/2 teaspoon ground cinnamon
1/4 teaspoon ground nutmeg
1/4 teaspoon salt
1 8 inch pastry shell

Preheat oven to 425° F. Beat together egg, pumpkin, sugar, spices, and salt with rotary beater. Spread mincemeat into the bottom of the pastry shell. Pour pumpkin mixture over mincemeat. Bake for 35 to 40 minutes. Serve with whipped cream, slightly warm or cool.

Brandied Pumpkin Pie

1 cup dark brown sugar
1 Tablespoon flour
1 teaspoon Ground ginger
1/2 teaspoon Ground allspice
3 eggs beaten
1-1/2 cups milk
Pinch of salt
Preheat oven to 450° F

2 teaspoons Cinnamon
1/2 teaspoon Ground cloves
1/2 teaspoon Grated nutmeg
2 cups cooked pumpkin puree
3 teaspoons Brandy or rum
1 egg beaten
Pastry for 9 inch pie plate

Line a deep 9 inch pie plate with pastry. Flute edges and brush bottom of pastry with beaten egg. Refrigerate. Combine sugar, salt, flour, cinnamon, ginger, cloves, allspice and nutmeg. Stir in beaten eggs. Combine pumpkin and milk. Add to filling mixture. Chill well. Add brandy or rum to filling; pour into pie shell. Bake at 450° F for 10 minutes. Lower heat setting to 400° F. and bake for 1/2 hour.

La Madeleine Pumpkin Pie

1/2 cup sugar
1/2 cup brown sugar
1/2 cup flour
1/2 teaspoon ginger
1 teaspoon cinnamon
1 (10-inch) unbaked pie shell

1/2 teaspoon allspice
1/4 teaspoon salt
1 can solid-pack pumpkin
1/4 cup corn syrup
2 eggs

Preheat oven to 375° F. Combine all dry ingredients in a small bowl. In another bowl, combine pumpkin and corn syrup. Mix dry ingredients into the pumpkin mixture. Add cream and eggs; mix until well combined. Pour the mixture in an unbaked, 10-inch pie shell. Bake 45 minutes.

Honey Rum Pumpkin Pie

WHOLE WHEAT PASTRY:

1-1/3 cups whole wheat flour
1/3 cup sunflower oil
2 Tablespoons ice water

1/4 teaspoon baking powder
1/4 teaspoon ground cinnamon

Preheat oven to 450° F. Thoroughly mix the flour, baking powder, and cinnamon. Mix in sunflower oil. Sprinkle ice water over mixture and mix well. Press the dough firmly into a ball. Then place it between two sheets of plastic wrap. Roll, from the center outwards, to 1/8 inch thickness.   Fit the pastry loosely into a 9 inch lightly oiled pie plate. Bake for 10 minutes.

FILLING:

2 cups cooked pumpkin pureed
1/2 cup milk
2 Tablespoons honey
1 teaspoon rum extract
1 teaspoon ground cinnamon

1/2 teaspoon ground ginger
1/4 teaspoon ground nutmeg
2 whole eggs
1 egg white

Thoroughly combine all ingredients with an electric mixer then pour filling into the pie shell. Bake at 350° F. for 30 to 40 minutes. A toothpick inserted halfway between the center and the outside edge should come out clean when the pie is done.

Apple Bottom Pumpkin Pie

APPLE LAYER:

1/4 cup granulated sugar

Teaspoon lemon juice

2 medium apples, peeled, cored, sliced

2 teaspoons all-purpose flour1

1/4 teaspoon ground cinnamon

Toss the apples with sugar, flour, lemon juice, and cinnamon in a medium bowl; place in the pie shell.

FILLING:

2 eggs lightly beaten

1 cup evaporated Milk

2 Tablespoons butter, melted

1/8 teaspoon ground nutmeg

1 pie crust (9 inch), unbaked

1-1/2 cups pumpkin, canned

1/2 cup granulated sugar

3/4 teaspoon ground cinnamon

1/4 teaspoon salt

Combine eggs, pumpkin, evaporated milk, sugar, butter, cinnamon, nutmeg, and salt in a medium bowl; pour over apples.

CRUMBLE TOPPING:

1/2 cup all-purpose flour

3 Tablespoons butter, softened

5 Tablespoons granulated sugar

1/3 cup pecans, chopped

To make crumble topping, combine flour, sugar, softened butter, and pecans in a medium bowl with pastry blender until crumbly.

Preheat oven to 375° F

Bake for 30 minutes. Remove from oven and sprinkle with crumble topping. Return to oven; bake for 20 minutes or until custard is set.

Pumpkin Chiffon Pie

3/4 cup milk
3 eggs, separated
3/4 cup brown sugar
1 envelope unflavored gelatin
1 teaspoon cinnamon
1/2 teaspoon nutmeg
1 10 inch deep dish pie crust shell (baked and cooled)

1/4 teaspoon ginger
1/2 teaspoon salt
2 cups pumpkin pureed
Sugar
whipped cream

Slightly beat egg yolks. Combine egg yolks with milk. Put brown sugar, gelatin and spices into a saucepan. Stir in milk mixture. Cook over medium heat stirring constantly, removing from heat just as mixture comes to a boil. Fold in pumpkin. Refrigerate until it mounds slightly (about 1/2 hour). Whip egg whites. Add sugar to taste. Fold egg whites into pumpkin mixture. Pile into pie crust shell. Chill until set. Top with sweetened whipped cream and candied ginger.

Impossible Pumpkin Pie

1-1/3 cup milk
1/2 cup buttermilk biscuit mix
3 Tablespoons butter
1 can pumpkin

Pumpkin pie spice
4 eggs
Whipped cream (optional)
1/2 cup sugar

Combine milk, butter, eggs, sugar, biscuit mix, pumpkin and pie spice to taste in blender. Blend until mixed. Turn into greased 9 inch pie pan and bake at 400° F. 25 to 35 minutes, or until knife inserted halfway between center and rim comes out clean. Cool. Serve with whipped cream, if desired.

Pumpkin Pie Surprise

TOPPING
1 16 oz. tub Frozen whipped topping

CRUST
3 Tablespoons sugar   1 teaspoon cinnamon
1-1/4 cups graham cracker crumbs

Heat oven to 350° F. In small bowl, combine all crust ingredients; stir until blended. Set aside 2 Tablespoons of crumbs to use for a topping. Press remaining crumbs over bottom and up sides of a 9 or 10 inch pie pan. Bake at 350° for 6 minutes. Cool.

FILLING
1 can Vanilla Frosting   1 cup sour cream
1 cup canned pumpkin   1/2 teaspoon ginger
1/4 teaspoon cloves   1/2 teaspoon cinnamon
1/4 teaspoon nutmeg   1/8 teaspoon cloves
1/3 cup melted butter

In a large mixing bowl combine all filling ingredients except whipped topping. Fold in 1 cup whipped topping; pour into prepared crust Spread remaining whipped topping over filling sprinkle with reserved 2 tablespoons crumbs. Refrigerate until well chilled. Best served cold.

Pumpkin Chess Pie

4 large eggs   1 Tablespoon flour
2 cups sugar   1/2 cup pumpkin, mashed
1 cup heavy cream   1/2 Tablespoon vanilla
1 cup butter, melted   1 9 inch unbaked pastry

Preheat oven to 350° F. In large mixing bowl, combine eggs, sugar, cream butter, flour, pumpkin and vanilla. Mix until well blended and smooth Pour into pastry crust. Bake for 40 minutes or until firm.

Cayenne Pumpkin Pie

2 cups canned pumpkin
1/2 teaspoon salt
1 egg, beaten well
1-1/2 teaspoons cinnamon
1/2 teaspoon ground nutmeg
2 teaspoons cayenne pepper (or less)
2 Tablespoons pecans, finely ground

1/4 cup honey
1 cup half-and-half
1/2 teaspoon real vanilla
3/4 teaspoon powdered ginger
1/2 teaspoon ground cloves

Ready-made pie crust or crust of your choice Preheat oven to 425° F. Combine all the ingredients in a mixing bowl, beat them together until smooth, then, pour them into a crust-lined 9-inch pie pan or ready-made pie crust. Bake for 15 minutes. Reduce the heat to 350° F. and bake for another 35 minutes or until set. Cool and serve topped with whipped cream.

Praline Pumpkin Pie

BOTTOM LAYER
1/3 cup chopped pecans
1/3 cup packed brown sugar

3 Tablespoons butter, softened
1 unbaked pastry shell

FILLING
3 eggs, lightly beaten
1/2 cup packed brown sugar
1/2 cup sugar
2 Tablespoons all-purpose flour
3/4 teaspoon ground cinnamon

1/2 teaspoon salt
1/2 teaspoon ground ginger
1/4 teaspoon ground cloves
1 can (16 ounces) pumpkin
1-1/2 cups half-and-half

Combine pecans, sugar and butter; press into bottom of pie shell. Prick sides of pastry with a fork. Bake at 450° F. for 10 minutes; cool for 5 minutes.

Combine first eight filling ingredients; stir in pumpkin. Gradually add cream. Pour into pie shell. If desired, sprinkle chopped pecans on top. Bake at 350° F. for 45 to 50 minutes or until a knife inserted near the center comes out clean. Cool completely. Store: in the refrigerator.

Irish Pumpkin Pie Recipe

1 9 inch unbaked pie shell
3/4 cup granulated sugar
1/2 teaspoon salt
1 teaspoon ground cinnamon
6 ounces beer *(You know what to do with the left over beer.)*

1 teaspoon freshly grated ginger
2 eggs
1-3/4 cups canned pumpkin

Combine sugar, salt, cinnamon, and ginger in a bowl. Lightly beat in two eggs. Stir in canned pumpkin and beer until well combined. Pour mixture into pie shell; preheat oven to 425° F. and bake for 15 minutes. Reduce heat to 350° F. and bake an additional 45 to 50 minutes, or until fork placed in center of the pie comes out clean. Cool, and serve.

Pumpkin Walnut Pie

1 graham cracker pie crust, 9 inch
1/2 teaspoon each, ground ginger, nutmeg and salt

TOPPING
15 ounces pumpkin, canned
2 Tablespoons flour
2 Tablespoons margarine, cold
1-1/4 teaspoons ground cinnamon
14 ounces sweetened condensed milk

1/4 cup brown sugar
1 egg
3/4 cup walnuts, chopped

Preheat oven to 425° F.
In a small bowl, combine ginger, nutmeg, salt and 3/4 teaspoon of the cinnamon, in a large mixing bowl, combine pumpkin, sweetened condensed milk, egg, Add premixed spices and mix well. Pour into pie crust. Bake at 425 ° F. for 15 min. Remove from oven.

Reduce oven temperature to 350° F.
In a small bowl, combine sugar, flour and remaining cinnamon. Cut in cold margarine until mixture is crumbly. Stir in walnuts. Sprinkle walnut mixture evenly over pie.

Bake at 350° for 45 minutes or until knife inserted 1 inch from edge comes out clean. Cool.

No Egg Pumpkin Pie 1

1 (15-ounce) can pumpkin	1 teaspoon ground cinnamon
1 cup low-fat soy milk	1/2 teaspoon ground ginger
3/4 cup sugar	1/4 teaspoon ground cloves
1/4 cup cornstarch	Dash salt
1 teaspoon vanilla extract	1 9 inch unbaked pie shell

You may substitute rice milk for the soy milk. In a large bowl, mix all filling ingredients, blending until smooth. Pour into crust and smooth the top. Bake 15 minutes at 425° F. Reduce temperature to 350° F. Bake until filling is set, about 50 to 60 minutes. Chill.

No Egg Pumpkin Pie 2

1 (15-ounce) can pumpkin	1/2 teaspoon ground ginger
3/4 cup sugar	1/4 teaspoon ground cloves
Dash salt	1 9-inch unbaked pie shell
1 (10.5 ounce) package extra-firm tofu	
1 teaspoon ground cinnamon	

Blend tofu in food processor or blender until smooth. Combine all filling ingredients and mix until thoroughly blended. Pour into pie shell. Bake at 425° F for 15 minutes. Lower the heat to 350° F and bake an additional 40 to 50 minutes or until pie is set.

NOTE:
Knife will NOT come out clean.

Pumpkin Cheesecake Pie

Layer mix
1 package 8 oz cream cheese
1/4 cup sugar
1/2 teaspoon vanilla
1 egg
3/4 teaspoon cinnamon
1 9 inch pie crust shell, unbaked
2 eggs, slightly beaten

Filling
1 cup canned pumpkin
1/3 cup sugar
1/4 teaspoon ginger
1/4 teaspoon nutmeg
dash of salt
1 (5 oz) can evaporated milk

Preheat oven and baking sheet to 350° F.

In small bowl combine cream cheese, 1/4 cup sugar, vanilla and egg. Beat until smooth and creamy. Spread on unbaked piecrust, in a medium bowl, combine pumpkin, 1/3 cup sugar, spices and salt. Add milk and eggs; mix well. Pour over cream cheese mixture. Bake on preheated baking sheet for 50 to 55 minutes or until puffy and sets. Cool on wire rack.

Dakota Prairie Pumpkin Pie

4 cups pumpkin puree
4 cups sugar
1 teaspoon salt
2 teaspoons cinnamon
1 Tablespoon vanilla

1 teaspoon nutmeg
6 eggs, lightly beaten
4 cups milk
1 cup light cream
Pastry for 3, 9 inch pie shells

Whipped cream and chopped nuts, for garnish

Combine pumpkin, sugar, salt, cinnamon and nutmeg. Blend in eggs, milk, cream and vanilla. Pour into pie shells and bake at 400° F. for 50 minutes, or until firm. Cool on a rack. Garnish with whipped cream and chopped walnuts.

Pumpkin Chiffon Pie in Chocolate Walnut Crust

CRUST

2 Tablespoons vegetable shortening
Real Chocolate Morsels

1 cup semisweet
1 cup finely chopped walnuts

Melt over hot (not boiling) water Semi-Sweet Real Chocolate Morsels and vegetable shortening; mix well. Stir in walnuts. Press over bottom and sides of a foil-lined 9 inch pie pan. Chill in refrigerator until firm (about 1 hour). Lift shell from pie pan; peel off foil and replace shell in pie pan.

PUMPKIN CHIFFON FILLING

1 cup sugar
1 envelope (1 T) unflavored gelatin
1/2 teaspoon salt
1/2 teaspoon cinnamon
1/4 teaspoon nutmeg
3/4 cup milk

2 eggs, separated
1 cup canned pumpkin
1 teaspoon vanilla extract
1/4 cup sugar
1/2 cup heavy cream, whipped

In large saucepan, combine sugar, gelatin, salt, cinnamon and nutmeg. Stir in milk, egg yolks and pumpkin. Cover over medium heat until mixture boils and gelatin dissolves. Remove from heat. Add vanilla extract. Transfer mixture to small bowl. Chill over ice bath until mixture mounds from spoon (about 30 minutes), in another small bowl, beat egg whites until soft peaks form. Gradually add sugar and beat until stiff peaks form. Fold moraine and whipped cream into pumpkin mixture. Pour mixture into Crust. Chill until firm (about 1 hour)

Honey-Pumpkin Pie

CRUST:

1/4 cup Plain bread crumbs	1/2 cup sugar + 4 Tablespoons
2 Tablespoons Honey	Water
6 Sheets phyllo dough	1/2 cup melted butter
1 teaspoon Vanilla extract	2 large egg whites

Preheat oven to 350° F.

Combine crumbs and 2 tablespoons sugar in cup. Place honey and 1 tablespoon water in microwave proof cup and microwave on High for 15 seconds. Lightly coat a 9 inch metal pie pan with melted butter. Sprinkle bottom pan with 2 teaspoons breadcrumb mixture. Place phyllo sheet in pan and lightly brush with melted butter, then, brush hot honey mixture over bottom, sides and edge of phyllo. Sprinkle entire crust with 1 Tablespoon crumbs. Top with phyllo; brush with butter; brush hot honey; then add crumbs. Repeat entire procedure to make a total of 6 layers, ending with phyllo and coating entire crust with honey. With scissors or sharp knife, trim dough to overhang by 2 inches. Fold dough under to form rim. Bake 12 minutes or until browned. Cool on wire rack.

FILLING:

1 package unflavored gelatin	12 oz Evaporated skim milk
1/2 cup sugar	1/4 teaspoon Cinnamon
1/8 teaspoon Ginger	1 cup canned pumpkin

Sprinkle gelatin onto 2 tablespoons cold water in cup. Combine evaporated skim milk, 1/2 cup sugar, the cinnamon and ginger in saucepan. Heat to boiling, stirring constantly, over medium-high heat. Stir gelatin mixture into hot milk until completely dissolved. Combine pumpkin and vanilla in large bowl; add custard and stir until blended. Refrigerate until mixture mounds when dropped from a spoon, 30 minutes. Beat egg whites and remaining 2 tablespoons sugar in a mixer bowl until stiff but not dry. Fold whites into pumpkin mixture just until blended. Pour into cooled pie shell. Cover and refrigerate.

Traditional Pumpkin Chiffon Pie

3 egg yolks divided
1 cup sugar
1/2 teaspoon ginger
1/2 teaspoon salt
1-1/4 cups cooked or canned pumpkin
2 teaspoons gelatin softened in 1/4 cup water

1/2 teaspoon ginger
1/2 teaspoon nutmeg
1/2 cup milk
3 egg whites

Bake: 1 Deep dish 9-inch empty pie shell until light golden brown. Set aside to cool.

Filling:
Beat the yolks with 1/2 cup of the sugar. Add the pumpkin, milk, and seasonings. Cook and stir in a double boiler until thick. Add the gelatin to the pumpkin mixture and stir until dissolved. Cool. Beat the egg whites with the remaining 1/2 cup sugar until stiff. When the pumpkin mixture has begun to thicken, fold in the egg whites. Pour the filling into the pie shell and chill before serving.

Wholesome Pumpkin Pie

CRUST:

1/2 cup unbleached flour	3 Tablespoons canola oil
7 Tablespoons whole wheat flour	3 Tablespoons soy milk
1/2 teaspoon salt	1/2 Teaspoon lemon juice
1/2 teaspoon baking powder	3 to 4 Tablespoons water
3/4 cup cane syrup	1/2 teaspoon sugar

Preheat oven to 425° F.

In medium bowl, combine flours, salt, sugar, and baking powder, in small bowl, mix together oil, soy milk, and lemon juice. Pour liquid mix into dry. Mix with fork until it holds together. Add water as necessary. Place in refrigerator for an hour. Roll out dough and line a 9 inch pie plate. Refrigerate until ready to use.

Note:
Try not to overwork the dough. Overworking wheat makes it tough.

FILLING:

2 cups pumpkin	1/2 teaspoon salt
1 cup soy milk	1 teaspoon ground cinnamon
1/4 cup cornstarch	1/2 teaspoon ground ginger
1/2 Tablespoon molasses	1/4 teaspoon ground nutmeg
1/2 cup honey	1/4 teaspoon allspice
1 teaspoon vanilla extract	

In a small bowl, stir cornstarch into milk until smooth and free of lumps. In a large bowl, mix pumpkin, soy milk, honey, cornstarch, molasses, vanilla, cinnamon, salt, nutmeg, ginger and allspice until smooth. Pour into crust and bake until done.

Seeds
&
Snacks

Pumpkin Seed Salsa

1 cup pumpkin seeds, shelled
1/4 cup onion; chopped
1 slice bread, torn
1 garlic clove, crushed
2 Tablespoons oil

2 Tablespoons can green chilies
14 oz. chicken broth
1/2 cup whipping cream
1 dash salt

Cook seeds, onion, bread, and garlic in oil, stirring frequently, until bread is golden brown. Stir in chilies. Place mixture in food processor work bowl fitted with steel blade; cover and process until smooth. Stir in broth, whipping cream and salt.

Roasted Pumpkin Seeds

1 quart water
2 Tablespoons salt
2 cups pumpkin seeds
1 Tablespoon vegetable oil or melted, unsalted butter

Preheat oven to 250° F. Pick through seeds and remove any cut seeds. Remove as much of the stringy fibers as possible. Bring the water and salt to a boil. Add the seeds and boil for 10 minutes. Drain; spread on kitchen towel or paper towel and pat dry. Place the seeds in a bowl and toss with oil or melted butter. Spread evenly on a large cookie sheet or roasting pan. Place pan in a preheated oven and roast the seeds for 30 to 40 minutes. Stir about every 10 minutes, until crisp and golden brown. Cool the seeds, then shell and eat or pack in airtight containers or zip closure bags and refrigerate until ready to eat. Yields 2 cups

Peter, Peter, pumpkin eater
Had a wife and couldn't keep her.
He put her in a pumpkin shell
And there he kept her very well

Toasted Pumpkin Seeds

2 cups pumpkin seeds
1-1/4 teaspoon salt
1/2 teaspoon Worcestershire sauce
1-1/2 Tablespoons melted butter or margarine

Preheat oven to 250° F. Do not wash pumpkin seeds. Wipe off excess fibers. On a cookie sheet, combine pumpkin seeds with remaining ingredients. Bake approximately 2 hours, stirring occasionally, until seeds are crisp, dry and golden. Enjoy!

Spicy Roasted Pumpkin Seeds

Preheat the oven to 350° F. Rinse the seeds clean of any pumpkin flesh. Combine the seeds with 1 teaspoon olive oil and 1 teaspoon Creole Seasoning (see below) per 1/2 cup of pumpkin seeds, using your hands to coat the seeds evenly. Place on a baking sheet and bake until brown and crisp, for about 15 minutes. Store in an airtight container at room temperature for 2 weeks.

Creole Seasoning

2-1/2 Tablespoons paprika
2 Tablespoons salt
2 Tablespoons garlic powder
1 Tablespoon black pepper

1 Tablespoon onion powder
1 Tablespoon cayenne powder
1 Tablespoon dried leaf oregano
1 Tablespoon dried leaf thyme

Combine all ingredients thoroughly and store in an airtight jar or container.

Roasted Pumpkin Seeds

2 cups pumpkin seeds
2 teaspoons garlic salt
2 teaspoons garlic powder
1 package Goya Azzafran Seasoning
1-2 Tablespoons crushed red pepper in brine
2 Tablespoons butter

Mix all ingredients except butter and marinate for at least 2 hours. Add butter and mix well. Place on greased cookie sheet and bake in a preheated 250° F. oven for 75 minutes, turning once.

Sweet and Spicy Pumpkin Seeds

1 cup pumpkin seeds	1/4 teaspoon ground cinnamon
5 Tablespoons sugar	1/4 teaspoon ground ginger
1/4 teaspoon coarse salt	Pinch cayenne pepper, or to taste
1/4 teaspoon ground cumin	1-1/2 Tablespoons peanut oil

Heat oven to 250° F. Line a baking sheet with parchment paper. Cut pumpkin open from the bottom, removing seeds with a long-handled spoon. Separate flesh from seeds and discard. Spread seeds on parchment in an even layer. Bake until dry, stirring occasionally, about 1 hour. Let cool.

In a medium bowl combine 3 tablespoons sugar, salt, cumin, cinnamon, ginger, and cayenne. Heat peanut oil in a large nonstick skillet over high heat. Add pumpkin seeds and 2 tablespoons sugar. Cook until sugar melts and the pumpkin seeds begin to caramelize, about 45 to 60 seconds. Transfer to bowl with spices and stir well to coat. Let cool. These may be stored in an airtight container for up to 1 week.

Pumpkin seeds can be roasted as a snack.

Toasted Spicy Pumpkin Seeds

2 cups pumpkin seeds
1/4 teaspoon hot pepper sauce
1 teaspoon salt

1 teaspoon Worcestershire sauce
3 Tablespoons butter, melted

Preheat oven 225 ° F.

Rinse pumpkin seeds until all the pulp and strings are washed off. In a bowl, combine Worcestershire sauce, hot sauce, melted butter and salt. Add the seeds and stir until coated. Spread out on a baking sheet and bake 1 to 2 hours, until crisp, stirring frequently to prevent scorching. Makes: 2 cups.

Pumpkin Seed Granola

4 cups oats (long cooking)
2 cups wheat flakes
1/2 cup oat bran
1/2 cup wheat germ
1 cup sesame seeds
1 cup sunflower seeds
1 cup other dried fruit
Any other interesting nut

1/2 cup raw peanuts
1/2 cup vegetable oil
1/2 teaspoon cinnamon
1/4 cup honey
1/2 cup raisins
1/2 cup currents
1 cup pumpkin seeds apricots,
    dates, cranberries, etc.

Combine grains, nuts, bran, and wheat germ in a big bowl. Slowly, heat honey, cinnamon, and oil until honey is thin. Pour over grain mix. Scoop into 2 large baking pans. Heat in oven at 225° F. for about 2 hours, stirring every 20 minutes until toasted. Add fruit and cool.

Pumpkin Blossoms

Pumpkin Blossom &
Chives Cream Cheese Spread

1 package cream cheese   6 pumpkin blossoms
3 blades chives, chipped

In a small bowl, work cream cheese until it is soft. Strip, peel, separate and finely chop pumpkin blossoms. Add to softened cheese along with chives finely chopped. Stir until well blended. Chill. Serve with crackers, bread sticks or bread squares (party breads).

Fried Pumpkin Blossoms

1 dozen pumpkin blossoms   Salt to taste
3 eggs   Pepper to taste
1 dozen saltine crackers   1/2 stick margarine

Pick male pumpkin flowers just before cooking. Rinse and set on paper towels. Crush crackers very fine into a shallow bowl. Add salt and pepper to taste. Mix eggs in a second bowl. Dip pumpkin blossoms gently into egg batter, then into the cracker crumbs. Because the flowers are tender, it is better to set them in the cracker bowl and spoon the crumbs over blossoms. Turn over and repeat. Place directly into a frying pan with butter or margarine. Cook until slightly brown. Remove from pan and place on a paper towel to drain.

Pumpkin flowers are edible.

All varieties of blossom are usable, but the Cucurbita maxima varieties, Hubbard and Butter ball, are more substantial adding more flavor and substance to your recipes.

155

Squash Blossom Quesadillas

1 burrito size flour tortilla.
2 ounces of fresh cheese, ranchero, jack cheese, or mozzarella
4 pumpkin blossoms.

Grate cheese evenly onto one half of the tortilla. Peel and strip the blossoms. Lay the blossoms in a curve on top of the cheese with their yellow tips close to the edge of the tortilla. Fold the other half of the tortilla over the blossoms. Finish cooking in the method you prefer:

Grill or in a frying pan:
Lightly butter or brush oil on the outside of the quesadilla. Cook until the quesadilla is lightly browned on each side.

Microwave oven:
Lay quesadilla on a large plate and build another quesadilla to fill the other side of the plate, cooking two at a time. Moisten the tortillas by wetting your hand and wiping the top layers. Cover and heat on high heat for one minute, rotate one half turn and heat for another minute.

Conventional oven:
Lightly butter the outside of the quesadilla. Bake at 350° F until the cheese is melted and the tortilla lightly browned. To serve, slice each quesadilla into four wedges and serve with guacamole, sour cream, yogurt, or salsa.

Pumpkin Blossom Soup

3 Tablespoons butter	3 cups chicken broth
1 small onion, chopped	1 cup half-and-half
1 clove garlic, minced	Salt and pepper to taste
3 dozen blossoms	Blossoms for garnish

In a large saucepan, melt butter, add onion and garlic. Cook until soft. Add blossoms that have been cleaned and chopped, stir until softened. Add broth and bring to a boil. Reduce heat, simmer 10 minutes. Pour mixture into food processor or blender and puree. Return mixture to saucepan, slowly adding half-and-half and season with salt and pepper to taste. Garnish bowls with additional rinsed blossoms.

Stuffed Squash Blossoms

Use your favorite bread or meat stuffing or stuffing below.

BATTER:

1 cup flour	1/2 teaspoon salt
1/2 cup cornstarch	1 cup beer, milk, or water

Sift together dry ingredients, then whisk in liquid until smooth. Cover and set in the refrigerator for 30 minutes. Leftover batter can be stored for up to two days. If it is too thick after refrigeration, add a few drops of water to return to original consistency.

STUFFING:

1/4 cup ricotta cheese	2 Tablespoons mushrooms
1 garlic clove, minced or pressed	1 Tablespoons basil
1/4 teaspoon each salt, pepper	or parsley, minced
Canola oil for frying	16 large blossoms

In a bowl combine the ricotta cheese, garlic, salt, pepper, mushrooms, (finely chopped) and basil or parsley. Open the blossoms and spoon about one 1/2 teaspoon of the mixture into the center of each. Avoid over filling the blossoms. Twist the top of each blossom together to close. Place on a baking sheet and refrigerate for 15 minutes. Pour oil into a skillet about 1/2 inch deep. Heat over high heat until a small cube of bread dropped into the oil turns golden brown within seconds.

Briefly dip each stuffed blossom into the batter, then, carefully slip into the hot oil. Cook until golden on all sides, about three minutes, total cooking time. Add only as many blossoms at a time as will fit comfortably in the skillet. Transfer with a slotted spoon on to paper towels and drain. Sprinkle with salt, if desired and serve immediately.

Note Pages

167

Index

Meat & Main Dish

Pumpkin on the Side
Vegetable Side Dishes

Soups & Chowder

Bread, Muffins, Cookies & Cakes

More Deserts

Beverages

Just Pumpkin Pies But Not Just Any Old Pumpkin Pie

Seeds & Snacks

Pumpkin Blossoms